**Haverford Twp. Free
Library
1601 Darby Road
Havertown, PA 19083
610-446-3082**
library@haverfordlibrary.org
www.haverfordlibrary.org

Your receipt lists your
materials and due dates

Online renewals at
www.haverfordlibrary.org
or
Telephone renewals at
610-892-3257

Enhance and enrich your
life?
Absolutely!

IT'S
YOUR
MOVE

IT'S YOUR MOVE

JOSH ALTMAN

My Million Dollar Method for Taking Risks with
Confidence and Succeeding at Work and Life

HarperOne
An Imprint of HarperCollins*Publishers*

HarperOne

HarperCollins books may be purchased for educational, business, or sales promotional use. For information please e-mail the Special Markets Department at SPsales@harpercollins.com.

HarperCollins website: http://www.harpercollins.com

HarperCollins®, 📖®, and HarperOne™ are trademarks of HarperCollins Publishers.

FIRST EDITION

Designed by Ralph Fowler

Library of Congress Cataloging-in-Publication Data
Altman, Josh.
    It's your move : my million dollar method for taking risks with confidence and succeeding at work and life / Josh Altman. — First edition.
        pages   cm
    ISBN 978-0-06-236925-3
    1. Success in business.   2. Success.   I. Title.
    HF5386.A544   2015
    650.1—dc23   2015001466

15 16 17 18 19   RRD(H)   10 9 8 7 6 5 4 3 2 1

To my amazing family—
Matt, Mom, Dad, and Heather—
for your love and support.

Contents

Contents

Foreword

Success is about ideas and relationships. Do you have the ideas to approach the world in new ways, push new strategies, and create new products, and do you have the relationships that you need to turn those ideas into a reality?

I learned these lessons pretty quickly because when I was starting FUBU I was basically broke. I had to practice, something I call, the "power of broke" and make sure I fully leveraged all of my assets and connections. For me, in the beginning, it was just asking my next-door neighbors to help me sew some hats. As time went on, it was the help and advice of my mom, my guy LL Cool J, and many others that helped me take FUBU from the basement to the penthouse. I understand and appreciate the importance of human relationships in the business world, and now, on *Shark Tank,* I try to return the favor by reaching out to entrepreneurs who are just starting out in business.

One of the men I know who understands the importance of personal contacts in business is Josh Altman. When we met in an airport a few years ago, he was forward, enthusiastic, and vocal about telling me how he could help my business. I meet a lot of people who claim to have "great" ideas, I'm on a show about it, but unlike many of those people, Josh Altman made sure to *show* me he could follow through on a handshake.

Since then, Josh and I have become friends, and I've come to appreciate how much Josh values relationships. He is always ready to lend a hand, and he understands how to create mutually beneficial deals. Josh is full of good ideas, but it's this heart that has allowed him to create a business with strength and longevity.

This book is a great compilation of the strategies Josh has used to make sure he is always on point and ready for those handshakes—to walk up to a stranger in an airport, introduce himself, and say "we should be in business together." It's full of useful advice for real estate, and business more generally, but it's really applicable to any aspect of your life. Confidence, integrity, and respect for your friends, family, and colleagues isn't just a business strategy, it's a philosophy. Josh's life and career are proof that that philosophy is a path to happiness and success.

—Daymond John

IT'S
YOUR
MOVE

Ready, Fire, Aim

America is a ridiculous place. Two hundred years ago, in a world full of rich and powerful kings, a bunch of farmers and businessmen thought they could run a country better, and then they did. Then generations of foolhardy people gave up everything they had to move to America on the outside chance they could make a better life. People born into poverty and slavery had the crazy optimism that this country was better than its past, and they believed that despite the crap that had happened to them, this was a place where they could build strong businesses and families. Women who were only offered jobs as secretaries after business school ignored the disadvantages they faced to work toward taking over the companies that had once rejected them. None of these people should have believed this stuff was possible, but they did.

America is a country built on confidence that defied the odds. That confidence was foolish, but it wasn't stupid. My goal in life is to be one of those idiots who see all the odds that aren't in their favor but still take the risk. I want to be one of the fools who make America great. That's what this book is about, and if you're a person who doesn't like to take risks, who just wants to keep your head down, do your job, and make money so you can pay your rent, you should probably stop reading, because this book isn't for you.

Okay, now that we've gotten rid of some of the dead weight, let's talk about confidence.

If the people who made this country great had anything in common, it was confidence. Despite poverty, war, and discrimination, they knew that the best thing they had to invest in was themselves. These days we live in a softer, nicer, more comfortable world, but it seems like people are constantly getting caught up in much smaller problems. Spending your life thinking about who is or isn't following you on Instagram is a great way of doing nothing with your life. America's greatness has always depended on smart people trusting themselves, but it feels like we've forgotten how. If you want to succeed in life, the key is confidence.

Confidence has gotten me everything I have. From meeting my fiancée to selling $20 million homes, it's only because I've known what I wanted and believed I could achieve it that I've been able to make my dreams happen. This rubs a lot of people the wrong way. They are threatened by me knowing what I want and how to get it. They call it arrogance. Look, when I was younger, I may have been a little brash, a little too confident, but I've spent the past ten years of my life honing my instincts to work in the world of high-end real estate. I'm not confident because I stupidly think I can't make mistakes;

I'm confident because I've made mistakes and learned from them. Despite what some viewers of *Million Dollar Listing* may think, what I present to the world isn't arrogance; it's informed, intelligent, *calculated* confidence.

Calculated confidence, to put it as simply as possible, is training yourself in your chosen field to the point that you can trust your gut instincts are guiding you toward the best possible option. It's learning, working, and listening enough so that when key opportunities present themselves, you'll be ready for them, you'll actualize them, and you'll learn from any mistakes you make in the process. It's making yourself your most trusted advisor.

It's not just about taking risks. Stupid people take risks all the time. Investing twenty grand with some guy claiming to be a Nigerian prince requires confidence. So does getting a "Subway Rulez" tattoo on your neck so you can get free footlongs for the rest of your life. That's the wrong kind of confidence. If you're going to take a risk, make sure it's a smart one.

Though if any companies want to give me free sandwiches for the rest of my life, let's talk. There may be terms that work for me.

Think about the gold rush. In 1848, a guy named James Marshall found gold at Sutter's Mill in Northern California. For the next decade, guys from around the world rushed to California to try to make their fortune. That was an amazingly brave choice for all of them. But how many guys made millions from the gold rush?

See, picking gold up off the ground isn't the biggest risk. It's a simple strategy. Everyone can see how that can make you money. Those guys found some gold and made some money, sure, but who made the *real* money off the gold rush? It was a guy who sold pants. Tailor Jacob Davis noticed that gold miners kept tearing their pants, and he approached Levi Strauss, who knew enough about clothing retail and San Francisco gold miners to realize the answer wasn't to just sell more pants like everybody else, but sell better pants. They saw a problem no one else was ready to see, they had the tools to solve that problem, and most important, they trusted those judgments enough to take a risk. "Oh, I had the idea for PayPal.com" isn't enough to make billions. You have to do it. You have to make the pants.

That isn't really the best business slogan: "Make the Pants." It's no "Lean In," but you get what I mean.

The risk those gold miners took was simple: they moved to California for a chance to pick gold up off the ground. Levi Strauss took a calculated risk. He took advantage of the opportunity to pick up gold where no one had imagined seeing it before: in the fraying pockets of those gold miners.

I've spent my life trying to be ready for moments like that one. A few weeks ago I was in the middle of finalizing a deal on the phone, and I said to my brother, "What we do here is 'ready, fire, aim.'" It was a joke, but the more I think about it, the more I realize it's also my philosophy. You have to be ready to identify opportunities, you have to have the confidence to make quick decisions and fire when those opportunities arise, and you have to learn from your mistakes and aim for better results in the future. You can be a success, but only if you train yourself to constantly be creating your own opportunities.

The most amazing day of my life was one of those "ready, fire, aim" moments. It started out the way most of my days start out: on a treadmill. I've been active my whole life—soccer when I was young, then in high school and college, and I still work out pretty regularly. In high school and college, it was mostly about sports and looking good, but these days, it's more about getting the blood pumping in the morning and making sure I have the alertness and stamina to take care of my clients all day long.

Damn, I'm starting to sound like a grandpa.

So it was a Sunday. I'd had a good weekend and my brain was pretty shut down, but despite the Friday and Saturday night cocktails still swimming around in my body, I noticed something: the guy next to me was somebody. He was a tall, good-looking, African American guy, and it took me a couple of minutes before I could place him. It was Tyler Perry.

I work in real estate, but I work in real estate in Los Angeles. In Los Angeles, all industries are the entertainment industry. If I recognize someone, they're probably famous, which means they probably have money, which means they probably have high-end real estate needs. Every celebrity I meet is a client I haven't signed yet. Tyler Perry is not just an actor, writer, producer, and director; he's someone I admire greatly. He's a mogul in the truest sense. This was a guy I needed to be in business with.

I was staring down at the treadmill, I was sweating, and I was wondering what I should do. A lot of people with a day as overpacked as mine was that day probably would have just looked at this situation as a celebrity sighting and kept going. I don't know if I was thinking straight or it was just the dehydration, but I couldn't let this opportunity pass me by. I was running next to a guy who was an amazing potential client. I had identified an opportunity, and I had to be decisive. A person can act or not act. Spending too much time considering a situation like this is, in the end, the same as doing nothing. So I reached over, tapped him on the shoulder, and said, "Hey, Tyler, my name's Josh Altman. I'm a real estate agent."

"Okay. Nice to meet you."

That was all I got. This guy was focused on his run; he didn't need me bothering him. It was an opportunity to walk away with dignity.

Dignity is for senators and bald eagles. I'm a real estate agent. I don't take no for an answer.

I said, "Hey, you ever think of selling one of your houses?"

I'm sure this guy thought it was weird that I knew where he lived. If Tyler had called the cops on me for stalking him, I would have understood. But I work in Beverly Hills: it's my job to know where the stars live. Plus, it means if real estate ever falls through, I can run one of those tour buses where you visit the homes of the stars.

He said, "Yeah, sure, for the right price."

That was it. Was it a commitment? No, but it was somebody who was interested in being interested, and that's all I need. Tyler finished his run, so I figured mine was over too, and I hopped off the treadmill. As I followed him into the locker room, I am *sure* Tyler Perry was starting to get more than a little annoyed. "Listen, Tyler, I've got tons of buyers who are looking for beautiful, modern homes with great views." I knew that's what he had. I wanted him to know I'm not just a part-time real estate agent–actor–bartender looking to squeeze some money out of a rich guy; he needed to know I was a serious professional who knew the market and could help him make a nice profit on his home. "Why don't I get your number? If I've got somebody and you'll entertain it, maybe we could make a deal."

I could have just sat on the number, but one of the first things I learned in real estate is that you should always have a house to show, or someone to show a house to. Intentions can fade, so the quicker you start the process of turning the intention into a deal, the better. I racked my brain, thinking, *Who do I have who might be interested?* I remembered a guy I'd been showing places to for six months. He was looking for something modern with a view in the $10 to $15 million range.

I called him up and told him that I had the best view in LA just waiting for him. I told him it was Tyler Perry's place so it was going to be great. He asked me how much Tyler was asking. I told him, "I don't know. Somewhere between $10 and $15 million?"

This guy didn't know exactly what he wanted. Tyler wasn't even really thinking about selling his place until I'd hit him out this morning. The house had been previously on the market for three years, but hadn't sold. It wasn't even listed at that moment. So Tyler probably didn't have a clear idea of what he wanted either. Why not try to help them figure out that what they wanted was what the other one had?

He said, "Let's see it."

I told him I'd make an appointment. He told me that he was only in town for a few days and asked me to make an appointment that day. So just hours after I had tapped Tyler on the shoulder on the treadmill, I was calling him up.

"Hey, Tyler. Josh Altman on the phone." I'm sure he was wondering who this annoying dude was who wouldn't leave him alone, but when there's a potential $15 million deal on the table, I'm willing to be a little annoying. "Tyler, listen. I know I just saw you, but I've got the perfect buyer for your place and I have to get him in there today."

Twenty minutes later Tyler's assistant was letting me and the buyer into the house.

I showed this guy Tyler Perry's 9,725-square-foot, four-bedroom, six-bath mansion at the end of a cul-de-sac in the Hollywood Hills. It was perfection, and when I had said it was the best view in Los Angeles, I wasn't exaggerating. My buyer said he had to have the place.

I sent the offer over to Tyler. He liked it, but he's a business-man. For some reason, when you're dealing with people for whom money is no object, they *always* negotiate hard. I guess that's the lesson: you don't become someone who doesn't have to care about money unless you always make sure to care about money.

We went back and forth; we negotiated. Tyler told me he was getting on a plane to go back to Atlanta. I knew that the minute he was on that jet, his brain would be focused on his produc-tion empire in Atlanta. He might intend to give his attention to the deal, but with the thousands of things Tyler Perry has to focus on, I knew that if this deal was going to happen, it had to happen that day.

As Tyler was on his way out of town, I sent him a number he liked, he agreed to accept it, and the deal was done. From seven in the morning until five-thirty at night, I double-ended an eight-figure deal. Ten and a half hours earlier, I was on a treadmill and I thought I knew what my day was going to look like, but I was willing to be wrong. Seeing an opportunity, pur-suing it, and not stopping until I closed the deal meant that I sold an $11.25 million home I barely knew existed at the beginning of the day.

That's what "ready, fire, aim" is about: being alert, educated, and savvy enough to recognize when there's an opportunity in front of you; being confident enough to make a decision in the moment and pursue it to its completion; and being wise enough to learn from the times your gut sends you in the wrong direction.

Let me be clear: This isn't just a strategy for real estate, and it's not just a book about real estate. The skills I learned for closing deals were built as much by hitting on girls in college as by selling houses in Beverly Hills. I learned to dress for success from my football coach, and my best investment strategies come from techniques my dad told me at the dinner table. These are skills I learned from real life, and they can help you in any aspect of your life. You're making decisions all the time about work, relationships, and family. It doesn't matter what the decisions are about; it just matters that you make decisions with calculated confidence.

You have to be *ready*. Life is short. You're never going to get what you want if you aren't ready to make big choices. You can't go through life waiting to feel ready. You have to be ready and know you're ready. It's a hard call for anyone to make, but I'm here to mentor you through it.

You have to *fire*. Life is about making decisions. When an opportunity presents itself, you shouldn't waste time. You should do everything you can to take advantage of it. In just about every situation, you know instinctively what the right decision is. The challenge is to not stop yourself.

You have to *aim*. Life is about learning from your mistakes and readjusting your aim. If you trust your gut and something goes wrong, you're going to be second-guessing yourself all the time. That's not the answer. The answer is to learn the lesson from your mistake and aim not to make the same mistake again.

Whatever your background is, whatever your skill set is, you have what it takes to be a success. The first step is to trust yourself.

You have infinite potential inside you. You have skills and aptitudes you haven't even touched yet. They're not going to magically appear, though. You have to create a set of goals and apply a structured plan to achieve them, but if you work hard and believe in yourself, you can achieve them. That's not false confidence, that's calculated confidence. And I'm here to put you on that path to success.

Part One

Ready

Every day when I get ready for work, it's like I'm preparing myself for battle. I know that I'm going to get into my car, and for the next twelve to sixteen hours I'm going to be on, pitching people houses, fixing deals, and making sure contracts close. When I'm in the heat of battle, I'm not going to have the time to ruminate on these decisions; I'm going to need to be in a space where I can trust my gut reactions. That's why that time working out, showering, and getting dressed is so important. I'm preparing for my day, thinking about what's on my schedule, but I'm also getting into a heightened state of mind, clearing my head of the unnecessary chaff from the night before, and remembering the kind of real estate agent I want to be.

Treating every day like a battle is the right idea, but a lot goes into a battle. It's not just about being brave; it's about having the right equipment in place, knowing your opponents, and making sure you fight on terrain that's advantageous to you. The same goes for business, hobbies, or any activity you want to pursue. The only way you can give it everything is to have the right strategy and ideas in place.

This makes it all sound pretty technical and military. It's not. It's just a question of giving yourself the best chance to succeed. Maybe you always get mad at yourself for not being the best, but how much do you actually do to give yourself that chance? You don't just turn around one day and get better. You don't go from not working out to having a disciplined, responsible workout schedule. You don't go from being a shy wallflower to being a great dancer. You don't go from living paycheck to paycheck to financial comfort in a moment unless you win the lottery, and a lot of people who win the lottery end up losing all that money and being broke again. Why? Because they weren't ready.

Readiness is composed of the structures you use to build your life. It's rhythms, habits, and awarenesses that allow you to maximize opportunities.

You want to start working out every day? Know yourself, know when you are most likely to work out, know when you're most likely to crap out and be lazy, and be honest about it. Know what your goal is. Give yourself a concrete objective: *I have to work out four times a week. I will lose twenty pounds. I'm going to make sure every desk clerk at this 24 Hour Fitness knows me by name.* When you know where you're going, it's easier to get there.

Find ways to love working out. Play music; make friends; flirt; don't use the machine you think you're supposed to use, use the one that makes you happiest. Any working out is better than no working out, and if you give yourself a positive feedback loop, you're going to create better habits. And stay positive, remind yourself constantly how achievable your goal is, and seek out situations that will help you on your path. Luck isn't random chance; it's work.

Tell people you're working out. Talk about it. You'll find workout partners, you'll find out helpful tips, and if you talk about it constantly for three months, when you get busy and feel like you don't have time to work out, one of those friends is going to call you on it. Be physically prepared to be the person who works out every day. Buy workout clothes you like. Have your gym bag with you every day. If you have the right equipment, you'll feel like the kind of person who works out.

And most important, be ready to face setbacks. Things worth having aren't easy. Let problems roll off your back and keep your outlook positive. If you keep working, you'll achieve your goals and life will get better.

When you're educated, prepared, and have a network of people who understand what you want to do, anything is going to be easier. I know you want to get out there and *do* stuff, but I assure you, readiness is not a waste of time. It's organizing and clarifying everything about yourself and your goals so that once you are out there doing stuff, you won't be wasting time, effort, or opportunities.

Life is short. You want to do the most you possibly can with it, so you can't afford to noodle around with success. Achieving your goals requires hard work, quick decisions, and big risks, and you're only going to be able to manage those successfully if you put structures in place that make you ready to achieve those goals.

So why not start now?

1

Know Your Gut

Never ignore a gut feeling,
but never believe that it's enough.

—**Robert Heller**

Human beings are animals. We're full of a powerful range of instincts evolved over millennia to keep us alive in the wild. Most people today ignore those instincts. They think they don't apply to our lives in a complex, scientific, urbanized world. They're wrong. Your gut instincts aren't the antithesis of rational thought; they are a quick, direct synthesis of the things you've learned, the things you want, and your body's physical reactions to the world.

This book is about being able to react to situations quickly, intelligently, and with confidence. It doesn't require that you be better or smarter than you are already; it just requires that you learn to use your intelligence and instincts together to make informed decisions quickly. Calculated confidence is a skill you can learn, and the first step is to get in touch with your untrained gut instincts.

Your gut is constantly sending you messages: *I don't feel safe. I am hungry. My boyfriend is lying about eating the last tamale.* Some of them are right; some of them are wrong. Getting on a plane can seem really, really unsafe to some people's guts, even though they intellectually understand that flying is one of the safest methods of travel. Throughout this book, we'll talk about how to manage the relationship between your head and your gut, but for now, let's just focus on being receptive to the messages your gut sends you.

Gut instincts are fundamental, animal messages. A lot of our gut instincts deal with stuff like food and shelter—the kinds of things we had to figure out before we were rational, thinking humans driving Priuses and living in townhomes. We can ignore these instincts as anachronisms, holdovers from our ancient past that don't apply anymore. However, if we ignore these instincts, we're giving up one of the most powerful tools we have for decision making.

Sometimes the messages your gut sends you are pretty clear. The summer before my last year of high school, I was going on a trip across the country with other teens from the East Coast. It was like summer camp on a bus: six weeks driving around between big cities and national landmarks. It was cool. There was fun stuff to see, some cute girls on the tour, and they kept us moving enough that we couldn't really get into any trouble.

Or so I thought.

About a month into the trip, when we were heading from the Grand Canyon to Hoover Dam, we stopped off for lunch and I got a burger and cheese fries. I didn't really understand it at this point in time, but my gut isn't the most tolerant of dairy products. We got back on the bus, and fifteen minutes later, I needed to use the bathroom.

There was a bathroom on the bus, but it wasn't exactly working. (After handling forty kids for a month, I'm surprised anything on that bus was working.) I wanted to tell the driver to pull over, stop the bus, and let me do my horrible business in some rest stop bathroom, but I was embarrassed. I knew that if I marched up to the front of that bus and announced I needed to drop a deuce, no guy would stop making fun of me and no girl would be interested in me ever again.

I waited. We'd have to stop somewhere, sometime. My stomach was telling me "sometime" wasn't soon enough, but I wasn't going to break. I was going to keep my, well, you know, together. My body was screaming out for me to ask the driver to stop the bus, but I just couldn't.

Forty-seven minutes later (you can sure as hell believe I counted), another guy asked if we could stop at a rest stop. The bus pulled in . . . I was so relieved . . . until I remembered I somehow had to walk to the bathroom. I tried to gently, gently stand up, and as I did, all the potty training my mom drilled into my head when I was three was useless. I was starting to lose control.

In the most awkward possible way, I waddled down the bus's center aisle, down the steps, and across the picnic area. With every step, a little bit more of the most embarrassing thing that'd ever happened to me leaked out. I got to the bathroom, said good-bye to that underwear, and did damage control as I hoped no girl had noticed my little bowel-control issue.

It was a simple, direct, physical instinct, but I ignored it, and I paid the price. Most of us have figured out how to pay attention to instincts that are fundamental by the time we're adults, but this book is about listening to all of your instincts and training them to be more sophisticated. The same instincts that tell you when you're hungry or tired can also process complex mixtures of data, judgment, and professional savvy to give you the quick reactions you need to be a success.

Your brain works more quickly and more subtly than you realize. Psychologists did a study where they showed people six pairs of numbers in rapid succession, then asked them which set of numbers was bigger. People got it right about 65 percent of the time. Then the psychologists showed them twenty-four sets of numbers in the same rapid succession. People were right 90 percent of the time. When there were only six pairs of numbers, people had to think about the problem. They did okay, but not great. When there were too many numbers to keep track of, people had to just trust their guts, and almost all of the time, they were right.[1]

Gut instinct is the biggest asset I have in business.

I recently got to meet a businessman I really look up to, Daymond John, the founder and CEO of FUBU and one of the investor-judges on ABC's *Shark Tank*. My brother, Matt, and I were at the airport in San Francisco. I'd just completed a speaking engagement, and we were heading back to LA. Matt spotted Daymond looking pretty incognito in a hoodie and sunglasses, *definitely* not looking like he wanted to be recognized, but I'm such a huge fan, I had to go say hi and tell him how much I respected his entrepreneurial skills.

Now, look. I may have been walking up to compliment Daymond, but I still took the opportunity to tell him that I work in real estate. I tell *everybody* that I work in real estate. I let him know that if he had any real estate needs, I could help him. He told me he was looking for office space in Hollywood, and I assured him I could find him a better deal than any other agent in LA. As soon as I was out of earshot, I was on my phone, setting up appointments for us to look at spaces. Daymond would only be in town for a couple of days, but I packed in everything I could. I'm a closer. I close deals.

We found a space that worked for him. The owner was asking in the low eight figures. I countered. We did the dance, we found our number, and Daymond was ready to sign the deal. I'm a closer. I close deals.

And then I did the unthinkable: I told him not to sign.

My gut told me it wasn't the best deal. Conventional wisdom would tell anyone that it was a solid deal, but my gut told me no, and I trusted it in that instant. I didn't spend a lot of time weighing options. I just *knew*.

What did I know?

I knew that this was commercial real estate. A house is all about your heart: it's the place you raise your family, share your Saturdays with the person you love, and kick back after a long day at work. If you find the house that's right for you, you know it. Commercial real estate is about your head: it's numbers. I knew that we'd seen as many places as we could in the few days that Daymond was there, but that probably wasn't enough volume to be able to find a place that was really *perfectly* suited to his needs.

What were his needs? Daymond's an entrepreneur. He's always got new ventures starting, and the place we were looking at didn't have the capacity for growth he was probably going to need. If I got him in the space, he'd be happy for now, but soon enough he'd be outgrowing it and looking for a new place.

I close deals, but I also serve customers. One multimillion-dollar deal will bring me a nice commission check, but an ongoing relationship with a money machine like Daymond John, in the long run, is worth way more to me. I knew that the best way to start this relationship was to put him in the space that was perfectly suited to his current *and* future needs.

I knew all that stuff, but I didn't have the time to think through it all, to weigh pros and cons. All those facts and pieces of professional expertise were like the numbers flashing in front of the people in that psychological study. My gut put them all together and synthesized them into a judgment without me rationally understanding all the pieces of the equation. The gut is the engine of calculated confidence. It powers you with instincts you have to be smart enough to train and understand.

The first step in training your gut is to understand yourself, your past, and the forces that shape your worldview. Your gut tells you the lessons you've already learned. It's the essential truth of all your collected experiences up to that point. My gut didn't always know how real estate works. It's been a long, slow, painful process of learning enough to trust myself to make the right decision in almost all situations. Training your gut requires that you look at the way previous experiences have shaped you and figure out how to supplement that with more sophisticated instincts.

———————

I grew up in Boston, Massachusetts, a rough, aggressive town full of big personalities. It was a world where aggression and being able to express yourself weren't just valued; they were necessary to survive. Boston guys have a lot of opinions, many of which they're ready to express with their fists, a lesson you learn really quickly when you're a kid. So from the start, one of my core instincts was to prove that I was a guy you didn't want to mess with.

My dad, Dr. Alan Altman, was an ob-gyn and a professor at Harvard Medical School. My mom, Judith, worked in the fashion industry. I guess they taught me the core lessons of my life: achieve great things and look good while you're doing it. Having a dad who achieved so much was a lot of pressure, but if you want to understand what real pressure is for a teenager, try having a dad who's a professional sex expert. Asking questions about sex is a bit intimidating when your dad literally wrote the book on vaginas. (Seriously, his last book, *Making Love the Way We Used to . . . or Better,* is available on Amazon.com.) Some parents teach you to work from a place of fear or doubt. Mine didn't, and for that I'm eternally grateful. I'm sure there are moments when they may regret raising me and my brother, Matt, to be unswervingly confident (some people even call it arrogant), like when I told them I was going to be on some Bravo show about real estate agents. I assured them the show would be great for my life and career, but they were skeptical. I hope four seasons later they share a little more of my confidence. I think they did a great job raising Matt and me. I hope they think so too.

And what about my brother, Matt? He's my best friend, business partner, former roommate, mentor, icon, and, for most of my childhood, primary sparring partner and bully. Matt's three years older than me, and growing up, I did everything he did. He played soccer, I played soccer. He became a field goal kicker, I became a field goal kicker. Then we grew up and went into real estate together. Look, there are totally times when Matt's opinions—always expressed very loudly—have gotten on my nerves, but I've always appreciated having a best friend around to give me advice and support. That's another one of my core instincts: anything I can do, I can do better working together with Matt.

Let's not forget my grandpa. He came over to this country from Russia when he was a kid, and he started selling stuff from a pushcart not long after. Pretty soon, he worked his way up to a (semi)respectable business in finance. And by that, I mean he was a hard moneylender. I'm definitely my dad's son, but when it comes to business, I take after my grandpa. He was a guy who solved problems for people. They needed money, and he got it for them. When people need houses, I get them for them.

When I was little, my grandpa would always tell me "Money is for lending, not for spending." I didn't always heed his advice, but the words stuck with me and provided me with one of my most basic understandings of money: it should always be working as hard as I am. That's a great quote and a great idea, but for me it's more than that. It's a gut instinct. It's something that was so hammered into my head that it is reflected in my actions without me even thinking about it. Investing just feels natural to me, and that's a good thing.

So what does the rest of my upbringing tell you about my instincts? It tells you that I grew up with hard-working, moral parents. I was trained from childhood to (pretty much) be a good person. I grew up with parents who always made me work for anything I got, so I'm going to be inclined to solve problems for myself. My upbringing also tells you that I'm used to having a mentor, competing, and trusting business relationships, and I'm going to be most comfortable going into situations that resemble my working relationship with Matt.

So maybe it's not so surprising that my fiancée is a real estate agent . . .

But knowing your gut isn't just about knowing what you're good at; it's about being brutally honest. You can only practice calculated confidence if you assess your good and bad instincts and are aware of them. So let's do it: let's talk about the ways my background can maybe send my gut in directions that aren't in my long-term best interest.

I'm not the tallest guy in the world. I'm five feet nine inches, which is a pretty average height, but it means I spent a lot of my adolescence and college years trying to prove myself: on the streets of Boston, in athletics, in business, and most important, to girls. As a guy with strong competitive instincts, I've got to be aware of when I'm going too far to prove that I may not be the biggest guy in the room, but I am the biggest *player* in the room. I have to know, love, and trust my instincts, but I also have to know which of those instincts are most likely to get me into trouble.

I grew up in a family of very hard workers; they taught me to work hard. That makes it easy to be confident, but it also means I'm not scared of some things a normal person should be scared of. I've fallen on my face a couple of times. I've taken big risks and they didn't work out, and in the process, my gut learned there are some risks to avoid. Whatever your background is, it's given you strengths and weaknesses, and you can shape those and build on them. Many people have overcome horrible backgrounds to achieve amazing things, and many kids with all the opportunities in the world never do anything, as you can see any day on Rich Kids of Instagram. What's important is to be honest with yourself about who you are, where you're starting out, and what it's going to take to get you where you want to go.

Your gut is constantly evolving, taking in what you've learned along the way. When I was twenty, my gut didn't know *anything* about real estate. It was making decisions based on lessons learned on the soccer field or hanging out with my boys. Those are valid skills, but the more you know what you want, the more you can focus and hone your instincts to fit your field. Knowing your gut instincts is the start. It will show you where you're going to instinctively push yourself in any situation. Calculated confidence is about deciding where you want to go and building instincts to push you in that direction. Following whatever gut instincts your background provided you with will make you an ordinary, regular person; shaping your instincts to go in new directions will make you extraordinary.

I had a decent upbringing, but anyone's background brings with it a huge volume of experience and training. We all have hardships. Maybe your parents divorced when you were three. Well, that probably means you've developed strong instincts when it comes to interpersonal relationships or managing multiple people. Maybe you got in a terrible car accident when you were twenty. It may have made you risk averse but confident in your ability to recover from devastating loss.

Your life is a treasure trove of lessons. You've been learning them and turning them into tools along the way. You just have to figure out what those lessons are and where your resulting instincts are leading you. Then you can try to shape those instincts to take you where you want to go.

Here's an example. I love soccer. Since I was a kid, nothing has felt as natural to me as that game, and it's all about instinct: knowing where the ball is going, knowing where your teammates are going, and knowing where your teammate needs you to be. I was good at the game because I knew what to do without thinking. I worked by instinct.

But I'm not a perfect soccer player. Soccer is a game of speed, and I'm not the fastest guy on the field. That doesn't mean I'm bad at soccer; it just means I need to shape the way I play to the skills I have, and develop instincts that push me toward using footwork and ball handling to avoid competitors instead of trying to outrun them.

I'm sorry. I never intended for this to become a book about ball handling.

The point is, when something is right, you know it. When you're good at something, you know it. Real estate is the right career for me because most of the skills it takes to be good at real estate are the same things I'm naturally good at. I could probably be a pretty good real estate agent just off of my basic gut instincts. Natural skills and passions are great, but they're never enough to be truly stellar at something.

I was never interested in just being good at something. I want to be the best, so I had to sharpen the gut instincts I developed during childhood, high school, and college into something a bit more focused. That's the difference between saying "Hey, dude, follow your gut" and the ability to apply calculated confidence to your objectives. The sharpening process is the "ready" in "ready, fire, aim." It's putting yourself through a kind of boot camp to train your instincts to take you in the directions you want to go, and to stop you from doing the stuff you find natural that holds you back.

You need to make success easy. Not just business success, any kind of success. Let's say you're someone who wants to get back into shape. When are you most likely to work out? Don't ask yourself when it's best for you to work out. Don't get mad at yourself for not being the kind of person who prefers weights over cardio. Don't get mad at yourself for not liking CrossFit. Start out by asking, *What's the way of making this good choice that feels most natural?*

Then do it.

Then do it some more.

Do you get super hungry after working out, then pig out? Make sure you've got healthy options *you actually will eat* there. Don't get mad at yourself for being someone you're not. Just know who you are, then find the ways to let that person be as successful as possible.

My dad gave me the best investment advice: invest in the products you use. Look, you're a magical and unique flower unlike any other, but you're also pretty average in a lot of ways. You watch some popular TV shows; you use the phone that's best and easiest for you; you drive an affordable car that looks good. So invest in that. If you believe in Apple enough to own an iPhone, buy some Apple stock. Clearly they're doing something right. Other people's guts are going to be as smart as yours, and they're going to make the companies with the good products successful. It's just that simple.

Jeff Bezos of Amazon has made thirty billion dollars doing just that: knowing people's basic instincts. Amazon doesn't just make shopping from your home convenient; it also *learns* about you. It finds patterns in when you buy and what you buy, then tries to make it as easy as possible for you to do that shopping through Amazon. It's called "predictive analytics," and it's the process of analyzing consumer data to predict behavior patterns.

If Jeff Bezos can learn about you from just a couple of Harry Potter book purchases, just think about all the behavioral patterns you can predict with a lifetime of data about yourself.

Learn what you do, then create a life where you're usually doing the best of what you do.

You have skills. Amazing skills. You have strengths the people around you take for granted and that *you* take for granted. I'm just a guy who likes to talk, thinks houses are cool, cares about other people, and isn't scared to take risks. I've been able to leverage that into a billion dollars in real estate sales. It's not about being the smartest, the handsomest, or the strongest; it's about having the right mix of head, heart, and gut to use the skills you have in the ways that are most advantageous to you and most valuable to the people around you.

I'm not guaranteeing you'll be a millionaire, but I'm saying you can be. And I'm saying you'll be a lot happier than you would be if you spent your life trying to fit into somebody else's model for success. If you're smart enough to find the ways your natural instincts can lead you to success, that success is going to be easier and more fulfilling. You'll be able to make high-speed decisions you can trust. You'll be able to see opportunities other people won't. The first step is just to step back, look at yourself, and figure out what your basic gut instincts are and where you picked them up. I'm going to show you how to sharpen those instincts into the confidence it takes to succeed.

2

Know What
You Want

Enough is enough! I have had it with these
[expletive deleted] snakes on this [expletive
deleted] plane. Everybody strap in. I'm about
to open some [expletive deleted] windows.

—Neville (played by Samuel L. Jackson),
 Snakes on a Plane (screenplay by John Heffernan
 and Sebastian Gutierrez)

Quoting *Snakes on a Plane* may seem weird for a book
that's about business, but it is, to me, the ultimate example of knowing what you want. There are snakes on the plane.
Neville wants them off. He's going to open some windows.
That is a business plan I can get behind.

Inaction is the biggest problem with America today. We spent the past century building the richest, most powerful country the world has ever seen, and now we're content to just waste our lives checking Facebook and watching *Duck Dynasty*. Americans have gotten lazy. The problem isn't one of skills or willpower; it's about goals. We're content. We've got food, shelter, and enough reality TV to keep us distracted forever. Too many people have forgotten how to push themselves to do something great.

The first step in doing something is to know what to do, and the first step in knowing what to do is to know what you want. The clearer your objective, the clearer the path to approach it is, the easier it will be to start down that path. The best movies all have a clear objective: steal the car in sixty seconds, destroy the Death Star, bang Stifler's mother. Once you know where you're going, you're in for the whole ride. If you spend the whole time wondering if you even know where the movie is going, the movie's probably not going to be that great. So, yeah, what I'm saying is I didn't really like *Vanilla Sky*.

But your life works the same way. The easiest path is a straight, clear path toward *something,* anything. If you know what you're moving toward, you're always going in the right direction. Clearing that path is going to be hard, though, because it requires you make a choice and let go of some of your other worries and desires.

Here's the simple, hard truth: you can't have everything.

Nobody has everything. The richest people in the world are either busy or worried that people only like them for their money or sad that they grew up without normal, middle-American experiences. Those are sacrifices. Awesome sacrifices I hope

I and my children will have to make one day, but it doesn't change the fact that, as the Notorious B.I.G. said, "Mo' money, mo' problems."

So you better make the thing you want worthwhile. Pick something good, because the more you want it, the more you'll be able to make sacrifices to get it. If you can't pick one clear objective you're trying to get to, you'll probably go nowhere.

That doesn't mean you can't change what you want. In fact, any reasonably intelligent human being is going to have their priorities shift over the course of their lifetime. Psychologists all over the world have interviewed people of various ages and found that as people get older, their goals shift from friends and education to family and careers.[2] My goals have totally evolved over my lifetime. When I was in grade school, my primary goal was to have fun. That's a simple goal. That's why kids are so happy. Before you can legally drive a car or buy beer, it's easy to keep things simple.

Then you grow up. One day, when my brother and I were in high school, we went to a local college football game. We saw the guys walk out of the tunnel in their uniforms as thousands of people screamed and cheered. Matt looked around, saw all the banners, TV crews, and, most important, girls, and he realized he was in the wrong sport.

"Dude, I have never seen girls get this excited at a soccer game."

"What do you mean?"

"I mean next year I'm playing football."

And that was it. What Matt wanted had changed. He wasn't just looking for a sport to have fun, he was looking for a sport to get him what he wanted: respect, attention, and popularity.

So you're probably thinking *Hey, being good at soccer and being good at football require pretty different skills.* And by "skills," what you really mean is six inches of height and fifty pounds of burly mass. And you're right, for most positions, but Matt figured out that a place kicker is essentially just a soccer player who only has to come off the bench for a few minutes every game. Matt's a life-hack king, and the reapplication of his soccer skills to football paid off in a lot more attention at school. I've spent my life following my older brother's example, so two years later, I had traded varsity soccer for varsity football.

I was a good enough kicker that college football recruiters started knocking on my door. Schools that wouldn't look twice at me based on my grades were now begging me to come play for their teams. It worked out, but once I was done with college, I realized I didn't really know what I wanted. Well, I wanted a lot of things: money; success; free time; happiness; an easy life; pretty girls to like me; a lasting, meaningful relationship; and lots of nice cars. This is a pretty common set of goals for guys in their twenties, which explains why so few of them actually achieve any of their goals. If you want a little bit of everything, you're not going to be able to devote yourself to achieving any of these goals.

Achievable goals need to be few, true, and intense.

With a divided, uncertain idea of where I was going, I had no clue how to get there, so I refined my goal to one simple, basic objective: I wanted to make money.

I tried, and I failed, but having a clear understanding of my goal meant I knew when I was going in the wrong direction. I wasted time at jobs that weren't quite right for me, but they were all stepping stones: selling phone service, working as a promoter at a nightclub, working the mail room at a music talent agency, assisting a TV producer. Even though these jobs weren't right for me, they were still valuable, because they showed me what I didn't want. As I spent time at each of these jobs, I started to realize they weren't allowing me to earn money based on my own level of work and intensity. They were (with one exception I'll talk about later) jobs that were about working within a company with possible long-term benefits but few possibilities to turn my own hard work into money quickly. They were interesting jobs but not ways of achieving my goal.

These jobs seemed like good jobs when I took them. They were cool and involved my interests, and when I had the chance to take them, my gut told me they were good ideas. One of the great things about gut instincts is that they evolve over time. The more you go through in life, the better your instincts will be at taking you in the right direction. (That's what the *aim* part of the book is about.) Your gut gives you simple analysis from complex data. My years getting yelled at by TV execs and music agents without any possibility of significant financial payoff taught my gut the kinds of jobs I should be wary of. After a few jobs I just wasn't a good fit for, my gut reactions shifted and started pushing me away from jobs where I was working for other people and toward jobs where my entrepreneurial spirit was the main determinant of my job success.

A clear objective changes the game. It makes amazing things possible.

One of my favorite stories about an innovative business is about a business that seems the least innovative: an old English house. Chatsworth House is the family home of the dukes of Devonshire, one of the oldest and most respected families in

British nobility. They're basically like the family in *Downton Abbey* except fancier (and with fewer sassy one-liners from Maggie Smith). Like the guys on *Downton*, they have an old, gigantic mansion—Chatsworth House—that has been in the family for centuries, along with other houses and farmland that make them one of the richest families in England. Times change, however, and even the business of being British nobility can require some innovation to stay relevant.

In the first half of the twentieth century, Britain was shifting from an old-school, aristocratic system with a big divide between the rich and the poor to a more social democratic system with socialized health care and other social safety-net protections for the poor. To pay for this safety net, taxes—especially estate taxes—rose dramatically. There were ways around the estate taxes, but they required that you be very prepared before someone died.

Which brings us back to Chatsworth House. In 1950, Edward Cavendish, the 10th Duke of Devonshire, was a healthy guy in his fifties putting the finishing touches on his will when his doctor came by for his checkup. What the duke didn't know was that his doctor was a suspected serial killer linked with the deaths of 163 patients. By the end of the appointment, the duke was dead of a heart attack and his will had not been properly executed yet.

So far this sounds more like a murder mystery than a business story, but it just keeps getting more interesting.

The Devonshire title fell to the murdered duke's son, Andrew Cavendish, but without the protections of a will, the duke's houses, land, and money were all subject to Britain's mind-blowing 80 percent death tax. After four hundred years, the dukes of Devonshire were going to lose almost everything. The new duke and duchess were still reeling from Edward's death and had no experience in real estate or finance, but they did have one clearly defined goal. They wanted to save Chatsworth House.

The first step was just to stop the government from seizing all their assets. The duke went in with an offer and a plan. He'd give Her Majesty's Treasury several of the smaller houses, large swaths of land, and a sizable portion of the family's priceless art collection if they would give him time to figure out how to pay the rest of the tax bill.

But it still didn't solve the problem of how these two aristocrats, who'd never worked a day in their lives, were supposed to make money. The solution came in the clarity of their goal: they wanted to make money to save the house. The duchess realized that the clearest, most direct path to achieving that was to get the house to make money.

Visiting English stately houses has been a common tourist activity in England for hundreds of years, but for most of that time, it was just a way for the upper crust to show off how fancy they were to the poor. The duchess, Deborah Cavendish, realized that they could turn a profit from showing off the house, and thereby pay the taxes and afford the staff and upkeep.

At first, the house was just an English version of Colonial Williamsburg. They turned their house into an opportunity to see how the nobility lived, they showed off what remained of their art collection, and they let people watch the old-school farming techniques on their land. As more tourists came, they identified better strategies for turning their home into an attraction. They added a petting zoo, then a shop to sell the food raised on the farm, then a tea shop so tourists could get lunch, then a high-end restaurant that served food raised or hunted on the Chatsworth estate.

Pretty soon, these income streams were dwarfing the money the family was making from admissions fees. They paid off the death taxes, and Chatsworth House evolved into a thriving business. It now averages over six hundred thousand visitors a year, grosses over fifteen million dollars annually, and, until her death in 2014, regularly featured the Duchess of Devonshire behind the cash register at the farm shop, ringing up customers.[3]

During the sixty-five years since Chatsworth House began its transformation, many British aristocratic families lost their homes when the changing economy made them too expensive to maintain. Some were seized by or donated to the government; some were purchased by people rich enough to keep them running at a loss. Chatsworth House has remained and thrived because the 11th duke and duchess had one clear goal—to keep the house—and they worked and innovated to make that possible.

You can do that too. Pick a goal, pursue it, learn from what goes wrong, and keep pursuing it until you get it. That's the clearest recipe for success.

---

can't tell you how many times I go to an open house that's run by a real estate agent who's pointing to living rooms and bathrooms like he's in a haze. He's acting like his job is just *being* a real estate agent, *acting* like a real estate agent. When I show a house, *selling that house* is my job. I'm not just trying to *be* a real estate agent; I'm *moving* that house. It may not seem like that big of a difference, but it's huge.

Give yourself the same chance to be successful. Pick a few clear goals and work hard to pursue them. Don't base your decision of a goal on what seems attainable; base it on the desire that's going to fuel you to do what it takes to keep going. Think about what you did in college. If you wanted to become a mechanical engineer and get a job for a major auto manufacturer, and you pursued that goal, you probably achieved it. If you showed up to "learn" but also "have fun," you probably drank a lot of beers and went to a lot of classes, but you don't have a lot to show for it. Think about where you could have gotten if you had just been clear with yourself about where you were trying to go.

Your goals don't just have to be clear and focused; they also have to be honest. Admit what you really want, because those honest passions will fuel you in a way that fake, obligatory goals never will. If I tried to be a professor like my dad, I'd fail. I wouldn't fail because I lack the skills; I'd fail because I don't have the right kind of desire pushing me. I love selling houses. Nothing gives me the same kind of thrill. That's why I can be good at it; because it's not just a goal, it's a want.

So what are the snakes on your plane? What do you want to do today, this month, this year, and this lifetime? And don't ask your head; ask your gut. It'll give you better answers.

When I got my first job in the mortgage business, my boss told me to put on the wall a list of the things I wanted, so I could always look and remember what I was working for. My list was pretty simple and materialistic: Breitling watch, Range

Rover, $2 million house. It's embarrassing now, but it was honest at the time.

Now my goals are less about possessions and more about building a life and family with the woman I love, but the things I do to pursue these goals, like working tenaciously at my job, are remarkably similar. Ten years from now my wants will likely have evolved even more, but what I'm doing to get them probably won't be that different. The want is about where you're going, but it's also the fuel to get there.

My moment of clarity was a condo. Some people learn their purpose in life in a message from God; I learned mine from a two-bedroom in West LA.

It was 2002, and you couldn't open up a paper without hearing about people making big money from real estate. Matt and I figured if we were going to be paying to rent an apartment anyway, we might as well put that money toward a living arrangement that would also be an investment. I was twenty-three years old, making seven bucks an hour in the mail room of a music agency, and there was no way I should have been able to get a mortgage on a house. However, it was the no-money-down boom time of American real estate, which was setting the stage for the 2008 meltdown, and Matt and I took the opportunity to invest in a condo of our own. We pulled together $10,000 from our savings and managed to qualify for a $400,000 loan. We looked at a bunch of places, and the more I looked, the more I wanted to look. Every condo was a different living arrangement, with different characteristics and opportunities. I was starting to get hooked. Finally, we found a place with a huge living room, high ceilings, three levels, and three bedrooms. Two single guys, potential to convert three bedrooms into two larger bedrooms. It added up, so we bought the place.

We put everything into it, all of our savings. There were probably the last bits of some money from birthdays and my high school job at a funeral home in there too. It was a big risk, but it felt right. We didn't know anything about real estate. I didn't even know what a mortgage was when we started. We just bought what we liked, but it turned out real estate came naturally to us. Our gut instincts were right. The place was a great investment.

The whole time we were living there, we were improving the place with every new paycheck we made. Every spare penny we had went into the condo, but investing all the money wasn't boring; it was the most exciting job I'd ever had in my life. We added wall sconces; we turned two of the bedrooms into a second master bedroom; we updated the bathroom fixtures and painted the condo. We turned it into a place we could be proud of. The area wasn't great, but any time my friends came over, I felt like I was the man. It wasn't just that I owned my own condo when I was twenty-three; it was that I was helping to shape it into a new and even more awesome home.

After six months, Matt and I realized the place looked pretty good, and we might be able to sell it and make some money. We listed it and sold it. Our $400,000 condo had become a $600,000 condo in less than six months.

If you want to succeed, you have to know what you want. In 2002, I finally knew what I wanted, and it was a life in real estate.

3

Fall in Love with What You Do

Choose a job you love, and you will
never have to work a day in your life.

—Unknown

My job is fun. Almost no one gets to say that. We live in a country of over three hundred million people, and most people spend every day at a place they kind of can't stand so they can get a paycheck that will allow them to have fun for a few hours on the weekend.

My job involves going to beautiful houses every day.

My job involves hanging out with celebrities, billionaires, and occasionally royalty.

My job involves talking to people, learning about them, and helping them find the place they need.

My job helps people build homes and families, achieving the American Dream.

My job lets me close deals.

I like my job, and that makes being good at it a whole lot easier.

This feeling isn't just possible when you're running a real estate firm in the best location in the world. Loving your career is possible in a lot of different environments and professions; you just have to find one that works for you. Knowing what you want is the destination; loving what you do is the vehicle that gets you there.

When I was growing up in Boston, I always dreamed of living in New York. To my little kid brain, that was where everything cool and exciting happened, and when I was in college, I spent all my time trying to pick up the trends and slang from the New York kids. I knew I had it in me to make it big in the Big Apple; I just needed my chance.

So the minute I graduated from college, I moved to New York. I really thought this was the life I'd been waiting for. I'd be able to be the guy I wanted to be: dressing nice, going to clubs, and being in the middle of the action. I got a job with a company that sold cell phone service to businesses, and I figured the only point of that job was to pay for my good times at night and on weekends. I had never realized how terrifying a job you're not good at could be.

See, this was a raw sales job, the backbone of consumerism. Every morning we'd have a team meeting, then hit the streets, soliciting businesses to buy our service. Our product wasn't that special. Our methods weren't that special. The only thing that could possibly be special in the entire game was the salesmanship, and mine wasn't that special. My first real job was the pure essence of the business of business, and I was terrible at it.

I would walk in and talk to business owners who had way more important things going on than to talk to me. I had no idea how to get their attention. These were real New York entrepreneurs too. Nobody's first language was English and everybody was pretty sure I was trying to swindle them. I have never been in a more hostile sales environment.

Here I was, living my dream, but it wasn't satisfying, because most of my day was spent working very hard at a job I didn't like and I wasn't good at. Sure, the job paid for some good times, but I couldn't help but feel like there was some way of making money by doing stuff I liked and was good at.

Some of those guys pitching the exact same service just *got* it. I worked with guys who were real salesmen for whom all these challenges were a pure thrill. The rush of a sale was a drug, and they would do anything to get their next fix. It was awe-inspiring to watch, but it wasn't for me. I wanted a job I could love that way.

Look, I'm a great salesman now, but that's because I deal in products I understand and love. I have clients whose world I understand and whose needs I can anticipate. I'm not a hustler who can sell ice to Eskimos, but if those Eskimos are looking for a sweet five-bedroom igloo with innovative architectural design and a heated indoor pool, I know *exactly* how to take care of them.

When I found the right field, sales came more naturally to me. The best way to fall in love with what you do is to find a job with major aspects that sync up with your natural skills and gut instincts, then use the satisfaction you get from those activities to fuel your growth in other parts of the job.

You know the show *Dirty Jobs* on the Discovery Channel? One time a fan sent a letter to the host, Mike Rowe, and asked him to recommend the right job for him. Mike shot back with a pretty strongly worded response, finishing up by saying, "Stop looking for the 'right' career, and start looking for a job. Any job. . . . Don't waste another year looking for a career that doesn't exist. . . . Happiness does not come from a job."[4]

Not to violate the ancient pact of solidarity between dudes on basic cable shows, but Mike Rowe couldn't be more wrong.

What does Mike Rowe do every morning? He wakes up, goes and visits guys doing awesome, interesting, hard jobs, and gets to leave before it ever gets annoying or really dangerous. His job is fun. Not everyone can be a TV host, though; it's a pretty frivolous job. Somebody's got to build the cars, fix the plumbing, and answer the phones. Those are all great jobs too, and there is stuff in each and every one of those jobs that you can fall in love with. Happiness can and should come from a job. I'm not saying a perfect job exists, but I'm saying your life will be better if you can build a career that you love.

Mike Rowe's argument that happiness shouldn't come from a job is just wrong. He's saying your job is just a thing you do to earn enough money to go have a good time somewhere else. That's the sad, paycheck-to-paycheck mentality that's been encouraged in our consumer-oriented society. It's a way to keep you as a piece in a game someone else is playing. Your place isn't innovative, creative production; it's to make money and buy stuff from companies that are in control. Mike Rowe's wage-slave mentality is a recipe to spend life struggling and in debt.

It's not even a recipe for real happiness. Psychologist Mihaly Csikszentmihalyi says the best moments in our lives are not the "passive, receptive, relaxing times. The best moments usually occur if a person's mind or body is stretched to its limits in a voluntary effort to accomplish something difficult and worthwhile."[5] What he's saying is that you're not at your happiest when you're sitting on a beach sipping a margarita; you're at your happiest when you're challenging yourself to try to achieve something you might not be able to do (like pronounce "Mihaly Csikszentmihalyi").

Like I said in the previous chapter, I rolled through a bunch of jobs on my way to real estate agent: J. Crew salesman, assistant to a TV producer, club promoter, funeral home assistant, mortgage refinance salesman. I'm a hard worker, and I did a solid job at all of them, but real estate was the first one that really captured my heart and imagination. After my brother and I bought our first condo, our real estate agent let me use his password for his multiple listing service. The MLS is a database that lists all the available properties in an area. The minute I saw it, I was hooked. It was a drug to me, like the way those guys from New York loved closing sales for the phone service.

It doesn't take being on TV or selling gorgeous Southern California real estate to have that spark with your job. You just need something about your job that turns you on. Maybe it's getting to be outdoors every day; maybe it's getting to talk to people; maybe it's working with kids who really need your help. If you find something interesting and rewarding about your job, getting up every day and doing your job to the best of your abilities is going to be easier.

You also need a job that challenges you, that gives you that Csikszentmihalyi sense that you're doing something interesting and worthwhile. Again, *any* job can be that job. It just has to be one you see that way. When I was working in the mail room at a music agency, I had a hard time seeing how me delivering envelopes extra-special well was doing anything to make rock stars more successful, but some of the guys there *did,* and that's what gave them the energy it took to be great at the job. From selling popcorn at a movie theater to creating new cancer drugs, if you can get hooked on the challenge of a job, you can be great at it.

The *best* way to fall in love with what you do is to find a job that's well suited to your skills and interests, but finding that perfect job isn't an easy task for most people. It's going to take a lot of time and persistence to find it, and in the meantime, you need to pay your rent. Luckily, walking into the perfect job isn't the only way to fall in love with what you do. The next best way is to focus on and expand the parts of your job that you do love. If you can't find the perfect job, work to make the job you have more perfect.

Every job gets annoying. It's a universal truth. The best thing in the world, if you get enough of it, will probably stop seeming like the best thing in the world at some point in time. How do you keep the magic alive? By focusing on the aspects of the job you enjoy and are good at.

I have a friend, Jason, who got a job as a junior high Latin teacher at a private school. He was a screenwriter who had gone too long between writing gigs and just needed to make some cash, so he decided to use his classics degree to get a job. It wasn't the perfect job for him, but he paid the bills and he focused on the parts of the job he loved.

Most schools don't teach Latin, so educational materials for teaching it are pretty limited. That meant Jason had to spend a lot of time coming up with his own curriculum materials. He liked that part of the job. He liked it a lot. He started out building slide shows, then animating them, then taught himself to program interactive games that taught the kids Latin, then algebra, then science.

Jason let everybody know how much he enjoyed creating interactive curriculums, and pretty soon the principal of his school was asking him to help with their technology development initiatives. The principal knew that they needed to update the way they taught, but he didn't have the expertise to do it himself. When he realized Jason was well positioned to help him out, he was excited to expand Jason's job to include more technology. Two years later, Jason's the director of a nonprofit program that implements interactive curriculums in public schools. By focusing on the parts of his job that he loved, Jason transformed his career and built the skills and résumé it took to get a job that lets him do exactly what he loves to do.

For me, the progression to grow my business in a direction that would make me like it even more was very natural. The more houses I flipped and the more money I made, the more capable I was to start getting involved with the high-end real estate in LA that excited me. I love taking a home, improving it, and finding the right family to live in it, but if I could do all that *and* get to hang out with high-profile people, even better. Next thing I knew, I was trading calls with NBA stars, Saudi princes, and the biggest stars of all: Kardashians. Life's been good.

Loving your job will make you happier, so try to find ways to love the annoying, tedious tasks that you just can't separate from this career that gets you excited. If you ask real estate agents what the most annoying part of their job is, most of them will tell you it's sitting open houses. You have to waste a whole Tuesday or Sunday just standing around a house, waiting for people to show up and take a look at it.

When I heard people complaining about open houses, I decided to make them my favorite part of the business. Yeah, you can look at it as a waste of an afternoon, or you can see it as the one time when people who are looking for a house are just going to walk up to you and say "Hi, can you help me?" It's the opposite of bum-rushing some poor shop owner and trying to sell him cell phone service. Even if I can't sell *that* house to an open house visitor, I can at least talk to them, learn about them, and figure out how to get them into the house they need.

So at my first real estate job, any time I heard someone complaining about having to sit an open house, I just said "I'll cover it for you" and snagged a couple of new clients. If we're talking about falling in love with your job like falling in love with a person, then that has to be the final element: liking the quirks. Some things are deal breakers, and I get that, but you have to either be invested in the career you have or find something else. There's no reason to stay in a loveless career, though. If you're going to stay in a job, you should love it and try to get everything you can out of it.

So the best way to love what you do is to find a job well suited to your skills. The next best way is to focus on the parts of your job you like, try to guide your job in that direction, and see the annoying parts of it as lovable quirks. Unfortunately, not everybody gets to have a job that takes full advantage of their skills and passions, but that doesn't mean you can't love what you do. Your job is part of your life, a big part of your life, but if you have to spend your time at a job that doesn't challenge and excite you, you can still find that actualization in your time outside of work.

We don't live in the 1950s. It's not like there are four corporations we can work for and the only way we can pursue an activity is to get a job with one of them. Information technology has created a world where we can pursue the activities we love and figure out how to make them profitable along the way. The Internet has made our economy flexible, adaptable, and mobile. That means you don't have to work a job someone designed for you; you can design a job yourself.

One of my favorite success stories is that of online entrepreneur Alicia Shaffer from Three Bird Nest. Alicia owned a small clothing boutique but wanted to add some headbands to her stock for Christmas 2011. She couldn't find any that matched the aesthetic of her store, so she made some of her own. They sold well, she made some more, then she started selling them on Etsy. They sold well there too—so well that three years later, Three Bird Nest was one of Etsy's top ten vendors, pulling in an average of sixty-five thousand dollars per month. Alicia ended up closing her brick-and-mortar boutique and focusing on her more profitable (and fun) online business.

Alicia didn't just grow dissatisfied with her career as a boutique owner; she let her career grow with her. She didn't even have to do it by taking classes or getting trained in a new job.

She just started doing something she liked and let people know she was doing it.

We live in a new economy with lots of exciting businesses like TaskRabbit, eBay, and Etsy that exist to provide a venue for your business ideas. Take advantage of them. There's somebody who hates doing the stuff that you love to do, and they will pay handsomely for you to do it.

It doesn't just work for businesses. E. L. (Erika Leonard) James loved to write, so she wrote Twilight series fan fiction. Even though she was just writing her own riffs on someone else's novels, her passion and talent came through, and with a few tweaks, that fan fiction became *Fifty Shades of Grey,* one of the biggest publishing successes of the past decade. Stevie Ryan did impressions on YouTube; she ended up with her own sketch show on VH1. And never forget that in the beginning Justin Bieber was just a kid singing on YouTube. Doing what you love may not make you a superstar or a millionaire, but it's going to make you happy. If you're happy with what you're doing, you're more likely to put the work into it that will make you a success.

If a career offers you spark and excitement, try to develop it in a direction that excites you and do your best to appreciate the tedious or annoying parts. A job you see as a burden, or just a way for you to make money so you can enjoy yourself on the weekends, is never going to make you rich, and it's certainly not going to make you happy.

4

Choose to Be Lucky

The best luck of all is the luck you make for yourself.

—Douglas MacArthur

'm a lucky guy. I grew up with two parents who loved me and showed me the value of a dollar. I had a great, smart, kind brother to be my role model. I was healthy and smart. I went to a decent school, but I didn't always take advantage of it. Above all, I had the luck to be born in America, a safe, secure country where people's success is based on how hard they work, not who their parents are.

I've been lucky in business too.

One time my brother, Matt, and I were early for a showing, so we had some time to kill. We went to a Starbucks because my most embarrassing addiction is Caffè Vanilla Frappuccinos. We were just standing in line when I noticed a very famous NBA player standing right next to my brother. That's luck.

Most basketball players are pretty physically distinctive. When a seven-foot-tall guy is standing in a room, you tend to notice, but this guy was a point guard, just a little over six feet tall, and wearing street clothes. Really, who would recognize Jason Williams or Steve Nash if you saw them at Starbucks? But for some reason, I recognized this guy. That's luck.

I went up and said, "Hi." The dude was very nice and said he was actually in the market for a new house. That's luck.

We showed him one house. He bought it. In one day, a random trip to Starbucks turned into us selling a $13.5 million home to a celebrity client, who appeared out of nowhere with virtually no work. That is a $337,500 windfall. It's like finding cash on the ground. That. Is. Luck.

Or is it? I could look at this story as a set of random events that lined up to make something awesome happen for me, but the truth is that those random events were shaped by the choices I've made in my career. I didn't set out to sell a successful point guard a house, but I created the conditions that made it possible. Let's look at the situation again.

Matt and I were early for a showing and we had time to kill, so we went to a Starbucks and an NBA player happened to be there. It's not random luck that put this basketball player and us in the same Starbucks. Matt and I were on our way to show a home to a guy who's trying to buy a $10 to $12 million home. We weren't at just *a* Starbucks, we were at *the* Starbucks, the best Starbucks, on Beverly Drive. In the middle of one of the most exclusive neighborhoods in the city, where celebrities live. Of course a pro athlete was there. If it hadn't been this guy, it would have been Kobe Bryant or David Beckham. I put my business where the high-end clients are.

I recognized this player. It is part of my job to know who my prospective clients are. High-income life in Los Angeles is my life. I love sitting courtside at basketball games and seeing the players on the court and in the stands. Of course I followed this guy on Instagram too. I need to know what the rich and famous are up to so I can anticipate their needs. In that Starbucks, I had my chance.

I said hi, and the dude didn't just brush me off like some random LA schmoozer trying to make some money off a celebrity. Again, not luck. I represent lots of people. Some are famous, some are just regular folks, but I've been around LA long enough not to be intimidated by famous people. I'm good at it, but Matt's even better. I think it comes from his years as a talent agent, but Matt has *no* fear when it comes to talking to stars. Someone like this basketball player can see that difference, and my confidence in the services I provide is apparent to anyone. The caliber of work I do is equal to the caliber of house a successful athlete would want to buy, so of course he's going to listen when I ask if he's in the market for a house.

And he bought the first house we showed him. Not. Luck. Twenty minutes before we were in that Starbucks, we were showing a client a compound in Beverly Hills. Our client didn't like it, but when this basketball player said he was looking for a compound, Matt told him that we had *exactly* the place for him. Even in LA, there aren't that many $13.5 million compounds. We know where they all are. We were the right people for the job in the right place to get the job, and we had the right skills to get it done.

That is luck. Luck isn't a random act of fate; it's a choice. The luck I talked about at the beginning of this chapter—my family, my upbringing, my health—those things are *actual* random luck, and I'm thankful for them every day. The rest of it, the seemingly random events that allowed me to become a success in my chosen field—that's the luck I chose for myself. Every day, in thousands of moments, you're choosing whether your fortune is good or bad. You have to surround yourself with the world you want to be in, be open to possibilities, and be willing to take them on in your own unique way.

If you want to get a lucky break, put yourself where the lucky breaks happen. Do you want to work in publishing? Move to New York; intern for a publisher; hell, work at the coffee shop across the street from a publisher. What matters is that you're making your intentions a reality. Am I starting to sound like some dude with a vision board? I'm no practitioner of The Secret. It's not like I have a poster-board collage of NBA players and a commission check, but my Instagram feed comes pretty close. The simple truth is that the first step in getting what you want is to put your thoughts into actions. Even if it doesn't seem like much, it's something.

Let's talk about The Secret. Some people dismiss it as *Us Weekly* witchcraft, a foolish attempt to solve problems with rituals and wishing instead of practical, hard work. I disagree. A vision board is just a simple, direct articulation of goals. I like that. Positivity is just allowing yourself to pursue those goals without letting your own doubt get in the way. I don't criticize philosophies or techniques; I just respect results. If your methods are getting you what you want and they're not hurting anybody else, I'm completely behind you. (Also, I shouldn't make fun of *Us Weekly*. I check that thing every week to see who just signed a big deal, because if they're making money, they're probably looking to move into a better house.)

That's how you create luck, by putting yourself in the world where you want to be. It isn't just about location; it's also about being the sort of person who succeeds in that world. It's about habits. I know what the habits are in real estate: answer emails the same day, always have a house to show, always let people know what you do, always check the MLS. Whatever field you're in, try to teach yourself to behave like a person who is successful in that field behaves. If you behave like a successful person, people will see it and notice it, and opportunities will come your way. If you behave like a successful person, you'll start pursuing and actualizing opportunities before you even realize they're there. In the same way that you can't wait for an opportunity to come to your house, you can't wait for an opportunity to transform how you behave. Be the person you want to be, and the world around you will take notice.

You need to be open to possibilities. Part of that is being humble enough to pay attention to the world around you. Yeah, you're important. Yeah, you have a lot to do. But so does everybody else. You can't be so certain about your schedule or priorities that you don't notice other stuff around you. Random shit's happening constantly. Pay attention. You may be able to benefit from some of it. Richard Wiseman, a psychologist who studies the idea of "luck," has found that people who take a more relaxed attitude toward life and are open to new experiences are more likely to have what seem like "lucky" outcomes. I'm not saying everyone should adopt a "more relaxed attitude," but he does make a good point about keeping your eyes open for new experiences and opportunities.

Optimism is a huge part of choosing to be lucky. You need to feel like someone good things happen to. If you're busy thinking the world is out to get you, you may not notice the opportunities to help yourself.

Professor Wiseman did a study where he asked four hundred people to count how many photographs were in a newspaper. About half the people described themselves as "lucky," the other half identified as "unlucky." The unlucky participants on average took about two minutes to complete the task. The lucky participants took just a few seconds. Why the huge difference? Because Wiseman had placed two large bold blocks of text in the newspaper that said, STOP COUNTING. THERE ARE FORTY-THREE PHOTOGRAPHS IN THIS NEWSPAPER and STOP COUNTING. TELL THE EXPERIMENTER YOU HAVE SEEN THIS AND WIN $250. Almost all of the people who identified as "lucky" found the text. Most of the people who identified as "unlucky" didn't.[6]

They're not "unlucky," they're clueless. The people who thought they were "unlucky" were playing by the rules. They were *just* looking at photos and trying to do it as fast as possible without paying attention to anything else. The people who identified as "lucky" left open the possibility for other, random factors to affect their outcome, and affect it in their favor. And it did. It can for you too.

Facts change, rules change. You have to be smart enough to see the change and be part of it. Rules keep people in a herd; you have to be ready to break out and act independently.

You also have to believe that good things can happen or else they never will. We had this one house that just wouldn't sell. We'd had it for six months, we'd tried everything, and there were just no takers. The owner called us to say that they'd already hired new agents who would be taking over the listing as soon as the agreement ran out the next day. Of course that afternoon we got a call. They were interested buyers, and they wanted to see the place. I had every excuse to assume that showing the house was a pointless waste of my time. I would have been totally within my rights to hang up the phone and not think about the house again.

Of course I showed it. Of course they bought it. That's how luck works. It's skill, work, good habits, humility, and optimism. Those are just a lot of words to say, so we simply call it "luck."

There's one final element that's really vital for creating your own luck that nobody ever really thinks about. You need to be you, and you need to be weird. Michael Mauboussin, the managing director of Credit Suisse, wrote a really awesome book called *The Success Equation: Untangling Skill and Luck in Business, Sports, and Investing,* and in it he says, "It is unlikely you will gain insight if your inputs are identical to everyone else's."[7] He's talking about stocks, but I think it's an interesting observation about human existence. It's a very dry way of saying that if you want extraordinary results in life, you have to bring something out of the ordinary to the table. Work hard just like everybody else, but the more you bring your natural skills, tastes, and talents to the table, the more likely you'll be to gain new, different insights into business and the world.

———

Luck isn't a magic answer to your problems that's going to fly into your life and make everything better. Luck is moving out of your comfort zone to run into new opportunities for success. It's making choices nobody else is making, seeing opportunities other people don't notice, and believing that following those opportunities is worthwhile. Luck is seeing the open door your skills, habits, and knowledge will take you through.

I don't want any part of this chapter to discount the very real and damaging random events people can face. Abuse, health problems, and random catastrophes happen to people all the time, and I can't remotely act like the fact that I haven't faced those isn't just chance. If you're someone who has faced this very real bad luck, I'm not talking down to you. I'm urging you to be brave and keep going.

It's easy to let negative events cloud the way we see the rest of our lives. Being beaten up by the world leaves you ready for it to beat you up some more. You can't give in to this pessimism, because, as Professor Wiseman showed, that'll just stop you from seeing the very real, very good possibilities that are waiting for you. However hard a life you have faced, you can make it better by choosing to focus on what's next and be positive about your future. You only get one chance at life. Declaring defeat at any point doesn't benefit anyone. You may be down, but you are *not* defeated.

I'm lucky. I've had a great life. I've had some real rough patches, but I made it through them, I learned from them, and I continued to make my life a success. You can too. The first step is just deciding that you're lucky.

5

Let Everybody Know What You Do

Without promotion, something
terrible happens . . . Nothing!

—P. T. Barnum

You're not alone in this world, but you're the only thing
you can really control. That's one of the roughest truths
of business. We're always having to rely on other people—as
partners, employees, or customers—and a lot of people, you
might have noticed, are assholes. Or lazy, or boring, or just not
interested in doing the kinds of stuff you want to do. That's
why one of the most important things you do in your life is
build a network around you. You can't just go through life

randomly collecting people. You have to seek out the kind of people who will make your life, your business, and you better. You also have to make it clear to the world around you who you are and what you do.

When I was a kid, I moved schools a lot. Four different schools in eight years. I was having real trouble with academics, and my parents were struggling to figure out the best ways for me to learn. That's not fun. My parents knew that I was smart and capable, but I was consistently incapable of translating that intelligence into the neat printing and organized arithmetic required of kids in third grade. I just felt stupid and insecure. I focused on the stuff I was good at—sports—and tried to get by at school as best I could.

The trouble was that I was showing up at a different school every other year. That meant I had to make new friends every year. That meant I had to let everybody know what I did.

Look, I was a kid. It's not like I had a job or business cards or anything, but I still had to communicate to other kids what kind of person I was. Also, I was going into this game as someone who had trouble with school. It would have been *so* easy for the other kids to write me off and think about me as some kind of reject. I had to make it clear to them from the very first moment that this wasn't an option. Nothing teaches branding like being a new kid in school with cognitive difficulties.

Growing up, *Saved by the Bell* was my favorite TV show, so I dressed like Zach Morris: jeans, preppy shirts, high tops that were unlaced. I knew that these kids did not know me, but if I dressed like someone they recognized, it'd be easier for them to understand where to put me in their heads. I talked about sports, I talked about people they might know from my old schools, and I flirted with the cute girls. I let them know that I was a preppy jock (who wasn't great at school), so they never had the chance to think about me as that dumb reject kid.

And they never did.

A huge part of success is people knowing you and knowing the best of what you have to offer. In real estate, contacts mean everything. One time a friend of mine asked me, "Would you rather hire a kid from Harvard with great credentials but no work experience, or a kid who never went to college but works his ass off waiting tables at The Cheesecake Factory?"

My answer was, "I wouldn't hire either of them. I'd hire a kid who grew up in LA." Every person I know is a link to more people in LA. In the same way I tried to find a frat that could help me reach the full limits of my getting drunk and having fun potential, I have to be looking for people now who want to buy or sell high-end houses in LA. Bring a kid who went to an upscale private high school in West LA to intern for me. That kid's cell phone is going to be full of people who should be my clients.

When I was deciding which real estate agency to join, it fundamentally came down to which agency most clearly communicated to me what they did. I was considering all the major Beverly Hills real estate firms, but Hilton and Hyland just kept standing out. It's all there in the name. Rick Hilton is a third-generation mogul. He's real estate royalty who went off and built a fortune of his own. And if I want to learn how Beverly Hills works, Paris Hilton's dad is the guy I want teaching me. Jeff Hyland is one of the founders of Christie's International Real Estate and an architectural historian with encyclopedic knowledge of LA homes and architecture. These guys had reputations that dwarfed the other firms, and since I knew what they did and how well they did it, I couldn't say no.

Most people have a pretty stodgy approach to professional networking. My network isn't just other real estate agents and people buying or selling houses; it's everyone in their world. My clients don't just exist when they're buying houses; they do a bunch of other stuff, and part of my job is to know about that. That's why my professional network includes people like the guys at Ferrari Beverly Hills and the jewelry stores on Rodeo Drive, agents, managers, producers, nail technicians, plastic surgeons, and divorce attorneys. Divorce attorneys are the best; they give you two sales, not one. That's where my potential clients are, so I want them to know who I am and what I do.

Recently, I got a call from a guy who wanted me to help him find a house. I assumed he'd found out about me from *Million Dollar Listing,* but it turned out he was actually buying a watch at a jeweler's in Beverly Hills, mentioned he was new to LA and needed to find a house, and the guy selling him the watch said, "You need to meet Josh Altman." That means I'm doing my job right.

Because your network defines and reinforces what world you're working in, but it can only do its job if the people in it know what you do. You should always, always be telling everyone what you do.

A great example is Airbnb. It's a young company that helps people rent their homes or apartments to vacationers for short stays. Since launching in 2008, the company has grown to five hundred thousand listings around the world, has investors like Ashton Kutcher and Guy Oseary, and is valued at $10 billion.

Not bad for a company that just helps people rent out their spare rooms.

Airbnb quickly built a brand identity, but that became its own danger. People saw Airbnb as a company that "helps people rent out their spare rooms," so when it tried to expand to provide additional services, like long-term sublets, people just didn't take notice. Offering a service wasn't enough; the company needed to tell everyone what it did.

Airbnb is very much a part of the social, sharing economy, so it knew it could get the word out through social media. It sponsored tweets on Twitter that announced the new subletting option, and it offered a discount code for two hundred dollars off monthly rents for up to six months. People responded, engaged, retweeted, and discussed the amazing offer, stimulating a 4 percent engagement rate for the promotion, but more important, solidifying in the minds of hundreds of thousands of people that Airbnb was a place to go to sublet an apartment or home.[8]

Social media is such a valuable tool for communicating who you are and what you do, but it's also a really dangerous way to waste time. I know so many people who convince themselves they're spending time on self-promotion when they're actually just looking at photos of high school crushes and taking Buzz-Feed quizzes. I, personally, use social networking platforms primarily to promote the business I'm doing. I don't have a personal Facebook page, I have a business page, and the feed is pretty much just houses that I have on the market. On Twitter and Instagram I occasionally post personal photos of Heather and myself, but I try to make sure these personal touches underscore my professional brand, not undermine it.

Social media also requires that you be aware of the image you present to the world. The simple truth is that we live in a world where what we make public on social media are things that we will need to answer for. Prospective bosses will be able to look through any photos of you doing body shots or lying passed out on a street corner in Barcelona. We're all human, and we've all had irresponsible fun, but you have to make sure that your online persona makes an impression that isn't at odds with your professional persona.

———————

If you're a real estate agent, don't do your job at the office. Take your stuff to Starbucks, sit at a table, and work there. Someone will come up to you and ask what you're doing. You'll get to tell them that you're a real estate agent, and they'll know someone looking to get or get rid of a house. In any way, in every way, you need to be getting out the message of what you do.

They call it the "elevator pitch"—that quick explanation of what you do and how you could potentially help someone out. People in entertainment and media are constantly getting it: here's a joke, here's an idea for a movie, you should write a song about me. Yeah, most producers, editors, and writers get annoyed by it, but that doesn't mean you should stop.

Back in the '70s, the carpenter hanging a door for George Lucas mentioned that he was an actor. Lucas had him read with some of the actors auditioning for a science fiction film he was making. Lucas liked the carpenter's take on Han Solo so much, he cast the carpenter, Harrison Ford. In the '80s, Michael Douglas had breakfast every morning at the same diner with the same waitress. She told him that she wrote screenplays. He asked to read one of her scripts. She gave him *Romancing the Stone,* and a few years later, he made it. Most elevator pitches don't end in a sale, but the people who are too scared to elevator pitch *never* make a sale.

I'm not encouraging you to be an annoying idiot. You can't just be enthusiastic about your message; you also need to be refined about who you're communicating with. That's what me talking to all those jewelers is about: if I want to work in a particular market, I must create that market. Starbucks is great for a real estate agent who's just starting out (or if you're at the Beverly Drive Starbucks in chapter 4), but I'm looking for folks who can afford expensive homes. I have to put myself where they are. If you're talking to a magazine editor or a film director about an idea you have, keep it subtle, don't be pushy, and let their interest guide the conversation. Everyone's going to be more engaged if they feel like they're discovering you instead of you forcing them to listen to you drone on about your idea for a novel for three hours.

That's why I fly first class. Yes, I appreciate the legroom, but it's about more than that. It's business (not business class). In any first class cabin on a flight between Los Angeles and New York, there is at least one listing for me. I can be certain that the people in that cabin are successful enough to do business with me, and they can be certain that my presence there means I'm good enough at my job to be taken seriously. My job is to get in that space and start talking about what I do loud enough that people notice, but not so loud that I keep Jessica Alba from being able to fall asleep.

I get it. Not everybody can fly first class. I'm not here to be a snob; I'm here to help you get results. There are other options.

If you can't afford first class, go to the bar at a fancy restaurant, order a glass of water, and start talking to someone who looks bored. Heather and I never make reservations, because that time at the bar waiting for our table is quality networking time. Drinks are cheap, and you're not there to have a good time; you're there to tell people with a lot of money what you can do to help them.

You set your worth. Just like when I would head into a new school, how you present yourself defines how people will see you. If you're scared of big clients, you'll never get them. Just the other day I was gassing up my car at a station in Beverly Hills. Let me tell you about this gas station: It's got a full-service option like it's 1952, it's more expensive than any other gas station in LA, and it is always full of people for whom money is no object. It is my happy hunting ground. I was at one of the full-service pumps and a fancy car drove up. Diana Ross was getting gas at the pump next to me. I'm not sure what grade of gas she was getting, but I assume "supreme."

I said, "Hi," then told her what I do.

Now, you're probably wondering how I can do that without feeling like the biggest ass on the planet. Like I said in the previous chapter, it's mostly about experience. Diana Ross is a legend, but I've sold houses for legends before. Matt's experience as an agent also makes him really good at it. The thing that matters most, though, is remembering that I'm really, really good at what I do and I can help them. I like to think of it like I'm a celebrity in real estate, and not just because I'm on *Million Dollar Listing*. In the same way that Diana Ross is one of the best at what she does, I'm one of the best when it comes to selling houses.

You don't have to be selling houses to VH1 divas to take your network seriously. You just have to think about what you're trying to achieve and what kinds of people are in and around that world. If you're looking for high-end real estate clients in the Midwest, you're better off knowing the staff at the nearest John Deere tractor dealership than you are knowing the staff at jewelry stores. It's just about building a connected network, then making clear what you do.

Information technology has made the world of networking even more dynamic. Now we've got LinkedIn for professional contacts, Facebook for social contacts, and Tinder for, well . . . you know. We've got so many more opportunities to maintain our social networks, there's no excuse not to take advantage of them.

One of my favorite stories is about a Canadian stay-at-home mom named Kelly Oxford. Her life was mainly focused on raising two small children, but she used her occasional spare moments to post jokes on Twitter. Friends loved her jokes, retweeted them, and eventually Kelly had thousands of followers, including a number of big names in TV and comedy. Even though she was working the never-ending schedule of a stay-at-home mom, she still found a way to let the people around her know she loved writing jokes. She contacted and cultivated her relationships with the high-profile comedy writers who followed her, and now she's published a *New York Times* bestseller and is an in-demand screenwriter.[9]

Yeah, five hundred thousand Twitter followers makes it a little easier for Kelly to get her message out there, and, yes, me being on *Million Dollar Listing* completely helps me out when it comes to broadcasting to people who I am and what I do.

I wasn't always on *MDL,* though, and Kelly wasn't always a Twitter megastar. The only reason I got to be on the show was because I'd talked off the ear of every one of my friends about how much I loved selling houses. One of those friends just happened to work in the same building as the producers of *Million Dollar Listing.* When they said they were looking for a real estate agent, he said, "I know a guy . . ."

That's all I want in this world: for someone to bring up real estate and the person next to them immediately say "You need to talk to Josh Altman."

The first step in succeeding is just to let the people around you know what you do, then never, ever stop talking about it. It's the thing you love to do, so the way you talk about it will be compelling, and the people you need to meet will be engaged by it. Am I saying that if you're a drywall contractor you should spend the rest of your life only talking about drywall? No. I'm saying if someone has a conversation with you and doesn't ever hear about how much you *love* drywall, you're doing yourself a disservice and a disservice to the guy you're talking to. His basement rec room is probably still unfinished, and you're exactly the guy who could have solved that problem. Self-promotion isn't an annoyance; it's letting people know that you're there to help.

6

Wear the Right Uniform

Vestis virum facit. (Clothes make the man.)

—Latin proverb

Suit up.

—Barney Stinson (played by Neil Patrick Harris),
How I Met Your Mother

've played sports almost my whole life. First soccer, then football. I did all right. I even got to go to a couple of Division I Big East Conference Championship football games. I didn't actually get to play in either of the bowl games, but it was still an awesome honor. I got to be part of a team and work hard with other guys to prove that we could be the best. Every time I put on my soccer or football uniform, I knew what my purpose was. It put me in the zone to give all I could on the field, and it let everybody around me know what I was there to do.

I still wear a uniform today, but now it's a custom-tailored suit. It may be slightly more expensive and not involve thigh pads, but the purpose is pretty much the same. So far in this book I've talked a lot about communicating to the world around you who you are and what you do, and wearing the right uniform for the job is about supporting and completing that message to the rest of the world, but even more important, it's about reminding *you* who you are. When you're wearing your uniform, you know it's time to get in the game.

Calculated confidence isn't just about an image you present to the world. You have to believe in yourself. That's not easy. Most of us were raised to be full of constant self-doubt. It's awesome when we see someone who really seems confident, but in our own heads, it can be hard to feel confident or act out the behaviors that broadcast confidence. I firmly believe that the road to confidence is faking it until you make it, to yourself as well as to other people. You need to remind yourself that you're a smart, competent professional, and that's exactly what a suit does for you. Your business uniform should be a reminder to yourself of your skills, intelligence, and training. And it should make you look and feel like a million bucks.

A good suit makes me feel like a millionaire, and if I feel like a millionaire, I'm going to act like a millionaire. If I act like a millionaire, the millionaires who are there to look at the house will listen to what I say, and if they listen to what I say, they're going to buy the house, which is going to make me money. Those suits are worth every penny.

But it's just a suit. Right? Of course not. A 2007 study in *Human Resource Development Quarterly* showed that employees felt more authoritative, trustworthy, and better at their jobs when they wore a suit.[10] It feels stupid. It's just cloth hanging on your body that's slightly different from the cloth you normally wear. But you also know *exactly* what the study means, because you too have had that experience of putting on formal wear and noticing the way it made you feel different.

It doesn't just work for suits. A study from Northwestern University showed that people who were given a "doctor's" lab coat to wear paid closer attention to data than people who didn't wear a lab coat. When the people were given the same coat but told it was a "painter's" coat, the increased attention to data went away.[11] The effect of a uniform on job behavior is clearly just psychological, but who cares? It works.

You guys remember Dumbo? That little mouse gave him a "magic feather" that let him fly. It turned out the feather didn't do anything but give Dumbo the confidence to believe that he could fly. That is magic, the magic of faking it until you make it.

You're probably saying, "But, Josh, I can do anything in any outfit. A hoodie doesn't stop me from believing in myself." That's true. It doesn't stop you from believing in yourself either. It's easy to forget about something if you're not being reminded to think about it. A uniform for your job is like an alarm clock for your professionalism. It reminds you that it's time to turn on your best.

A suit doesn't just change your mind-set; it actually changes the quality of the work you do. You ready for another study? The *Journal of Applied Psychology* found that people wearing suits "used more formal adjectives than casual ones to describe themselves . . . [and] responded faster to formal than to casual adjectives."[12] When you're in a suit, you're shifting the way you see yourself, and that's going to make a positive impression on anyone you're working with.

In 1995, Nancy Lublin inherited five thousand dollars from her grandfather. Nancy's a socially minded person, and she wanted to figure out a way to make that money give back to society while honoring her grandfather's memory. She went to a shelter for women and asked how she could help. The social workers said the women had professional skills but not the professional clothes to get taken seriously at interviews. Nancy used that five thousand dollars to found Dress for Success, a nonprofit organization that provides suits to underprivileged women looking for work, then an additional suit and separates to be able to dress professionally for a full week once they get a job.[13]

Every year, Dress for Success helps over seven hundred thousand women around the world go from dependence on charity and government aid to self-sufficiency in the business world. The difference isn't job skills or child care; the difference is as simple and profound as a suit. And it works.

When I started in real estate, I was younger than most of the guys in the job. I needed a way to make myself seem a little bit more experienced and respectable. The answer was a good, well-tailored suit. I wasn't just some kid; I was a businessman.

Now I've been in the real estate game for a long time, and I've had a lot of success. I don't need to bolster my confidence or try to seem older, but I still wear a suit every day because every little reminder that I should take myself seriously helps. It's almost like one of my favorite movies, *Limitless,* in which

Bradley Cooper's character takes a pill to make him smarter. My suits are the magic pills that keep me confident all day long. Who doesn't want the benefits of a performance-enhancing drug, especially when I look so good in it?

Seriously, though, my suits are about sending myself a complex message. They're expensive. That reminds me that I'm a success and I will continue to be a success. My suits are tailored to me, which just gives me the ease and confidence that comes with everything fitting right and looking good. Mostly, though, my suits are something my fiancée, Heather, picks out for me. She has a little message stitched into each one, like "Property of Heather" or "Calculated Confidence." The suits are a reminder that I have someone who loves me, respects me, and wants me to succeed. It may not be armor, but it makes me feel invincible.

When I started in LA real estate, things were very laid back and casual. This is California: a lot of business gets done in flip-flops and shorts. I wanted to bring some East Coast swagger to the game to let people know that I was not relaxed about getting them the best deal. It worked, and now there are a lot more real estate agents dressing a lot better in LA.

There are other ways to communicate professionalism, but don't assume everybody will be able to notice them. I've been in the real estate game for a long time, and a smart person should be able to recognize my skills from the way I do my job, but not every client is smart. I don't *need* them to be smart; I just need them to be able to afford a $5 million house. I'm not going to hope they notice who I am; I'm going to tell them who I am with everything I do. Don't give people the chance not to realize who you are. They may just take it.

Just because I'm telling you to create your own uniform for work doesn't mean I'm telling you to conform, not at all. Your uniform doesn't need to be the same as everybody else's; you just need to think honestly about the message your uniform sends to other people. Not fitting in has its advantages, actually. If you were worried that this meant I was going to quote another study, you were right.

The *Journal of Consumer Research* found that people associate nonconformity with power. They showed people a photo of a bunch of men in tuxedos at a country club. All the men had black ties except for one man, who had a red tie. The people assumed the guy in the red tie must be special: a top member of the club, the winner of more golf tournaments, or just more creative. Red is a deeply powerful color too. A recent survey of CEOs found they were most attracted to the color red. I guess red doesn't just attract bulls; it attracts bull markets.[14]

That's why I like to occasionally wear suits with a sharkskin sheen to them, or with ties or pocket squares that give it some color. I want people, and myself, to see the authority and care that goes into my outfit, but I also want them to know that I'm not just another mediocre real estate agent. I'm willing to stand out. I'm a predator, not prey.

You don't have to put on a three-thousand-dollar suit to be dressed for success. Suits aren't about how much they cost; they're mostly about respect. It shows that you take yourself and your clients seriously. You can never be overdressed to do business, but you can be underdressed. Once a client sees you in a T-shirt or jeans, they're going to stop thinking of you as a single-purpose real estate machine and just start thinking of you as a person. Nobody wants that.

You can afford to wear a suit and look good in it. When I first started out in real estate, I had one suit to wear to weddings and funerals. I realized that wasn't going to cut it in this business, so I went to Men's Wearhouse and got three suits, three belts, and three pairs of socks for three hundred and thirty-three dollars. They weren't the finest suits in the world—in fact, they were polyester—but they reminded me that I was a pro, and I did better work because of that. Oh, and here's a tip: however much or little you paid for your suit, go to a tailor and get it tailored to fit you. It's not that expensive, but it starts sending the message that you're to be taken seriously. I promise you that suit will pay for itself, and a fancier replacement, within a year.

The important thing about a suit is that you look natural in it. Your suit should communicate how comfortable you are in your role in business. If you are wearing a suit that doesn't fit, people are going to assume you're in a job that doesn't fit you either. We're so used to buying clothes off the rack that we may think of tailors as some kind of anachronism. They're not. They're amazing men and women who make clothes fit you correctly and effortlessly. When you're standing in that suit with the perfect break and sleeves that are just the right length, you're going to remind everyone, including yourself, how ready for the job you are.

Ties also send a big message. Bold colors make it impossible for people to ignore your presence, and I always use a double Windsor knot. It's a thick, substantial knot that lets people know I'm serious. There are lots of videos on YouTube that'll teach you to tie a double Windsor. Go take a look. It's worth your time to make sure you look like someone who matters.

I don't see Donald Trump or Barack Obama wearing skinny ties, so I'm not going to either.

You don't have to follow my lead. It's style, and you're going to make the choices that are right for you. You have to take that style seriously, though, and be honest with yourself about the message that choice is sending and who it's telling the world you are.

Also, a pocket square wouldn't hurt.

It's about balance too. I always try to go with a suit that's trustworthy and a tie that's noteworthy. I want my main message to be that I know what I'm doing and how to play the game, but I present it with enough splash of color that people know I'm not scared of risks.

I know this chapter can seem inapplicable to women. I've been talking about men's business suits a lot, but the truth is, this subject is even more important for women. For a long time women were largely excluded from professional life, but after a hard fight to be taken seriously, women are now making a major impact in the business world. A problem that comes along with this is that men know what they're supposed to wear into an office, but for women, it's a constant, uncertain question. Minor mistakes can give men the excuse they're looking for to disregard or disrespect you. It is most important that a woman in business be wearing a uniform that reminds her colleagues and herself that she's to be taken seriously.

Women don't have hundreds of years of tradition with business clothes; they've got like forty. It means women have more questions to ask: skirt or pants, color or no color, and how much they should lady it up with jewelry, heels, or that fabulous designer purse.

It's interesting to watch my fiancée, Heather, negotiate that question. She's great at tweaking the message she's sending with her outfit to accommodate the situations presented to her. One day last week, she left the house looking amazing: high heels, hair down, great suit. She was showing a condo to a young, single, professional man. When I saw her at lunch, her hair was up. I asked why, and she told me she'd been showing houses to a couple in their thirties and didn't want to seem too sexual. A couple of hours later, she was pulling tennis shoes out of the back of her car so we could walk around the dirt and concrete at a development site.

Heather's job requires that she be able to present different uniforms at different times, and she takes it seriously. She always has five pairs of shoes in her car, because her day could involve a range of events from upscale lunches to walking through drainage ditches. She's ready for all of it, and so is her uniform.

———

All this suit talk has been pretty clearly targeted to people whose goals revolve around business and career. If your goal is to be an amazing gymnast, wearing a power suit and a red tie probably won't be the best way to tell the opposing athletes they need to take you seriously. But the core message of this chapter—that you should wear the right uniform for the job you want to do—doesn't stop being true just because the uniform is different.

If your goal is to get a girlfriend, you should still have a uniform. Every time you go on a date, you should put on an outfit that lets you know you're going into the game: an outfit that looks good and reminds you to keep your anecdote game tight. If your goal is to grow the best damned tomatoes you've ever grown, get a pair of new gardening gloves and love them. Every time you look at them, think about the kick-ass gardener you are when you have them on. And get a pair that fits you perfectly and feels fantastic when you are wearing them while gardening. Like all those studies told us, clothes are about appearance, but they're mostly about psychology. You need to make the psychology work for you.

This book is about calculated confidence, being prepared to believe in yourself in high-pressure situations. Just about everything else in the book will be about the calculations: knowing how to be smart and ready for decisions. This chapter is almost entirely about the confidence. A uniform is just a way to put you into the zone to feel like you're working at your highest capacity. It doesn't have to be a suit. Whatever magic feather gives you confidence, use it.

Some people will call it a crutch. They're not wrong. I just don't think a crutch is a terrible thing when you're learning to walk, or, in this case, be confident.

Symbolism is useful. It's easy to crap on people for wearing a peace sign, having a team jersey, or getting their mom's name tattooed on them. It seems silly that you'd need a reminder to make you think about peace, where you're from, or your mom. But it helps, and that matters.

Confidence is even harder, because it's a constant fight. Every little mistake is an opportunity for you to lose faith in yourself and give up. If you just decide to be confident, you can decide not to be just as quickly. That suit is there to remind you that when you got ready that morning, you made a commitment to believe in yourself all day long. Stick to that commitment, because it's worth it.

You are constantly and consistently the greatest investment you're ever going to make, and it's a long-term investment. You can't just sell you and buy stock in another person. You need to support and insure that investment to maximize its potential.

What I'm saying is buy a damn suit.

7

Have a Tough Skin

Never give in. Never give in. Never, never, never, never—in nothing, great or small, large or petty—never give in, except to convictions of honor and good sense.

—Winston Churchill

Life is hard. You have faced and will face obstacles that will make you want to give up on your goals. Your hopes will not come true, your fears will come true, and the people you rely on will fail you. All of this stuff is going to happen, but you are strong enough to make it through. If you let these hard times stop you, you will fail, but if you let the world come at you with all of its danger and difficulty and you keep fighting, no one can stop you.

There have been dozens of deals where I got cheated out of a commission. There will be dozens more deals where I get cheated out of a commission. That's no reason to give up, and it's no reason to ignore all the satisfaction my career has brought me. Negative experiences may contain valuable lessons, but they are mainly just distractions from your path. You have to keep moving. You have to ignore the small stuff if you want to be a success. You have to be strong. Every one of us has the capacity to be that strong.

Homes are the biggest investment in most people's lives. That means they have a huge meaning, both financially and emotionally. It's one of the things that make me love my job. It also brings out the worst in people. Clients of mine who are perfectly nice people in every other aspect of their lives can turn into complete monsters when it comes time to buy or sell a house. That's one of the dangers of my chosen field, so I have to learn to not let it bother me.

I had a client who had made a billion dollars making toys. His hobby is real estate development. You'd think that a guy with more money than God, pursuing development as a hobby, would be a really chill guy to deal with. You would be wrong. This guy didn't make it to the top of the toy industry by being chill, and he brings that same level of intensity to his development business. He's got a vision, a team of all-stars to execute that vision, and stringent standards for getting it done right. He was never easy to work with, but I was excited to be part of his process. He's just a hobbyist, but he's crushing it harder than the pros.

So I located a property for him, a $9 million tear-down in Brentwood. I convinced him to buy the property, and I watched as he transformed it into a home that was easily worth double that price. I stopped by every few weeks or so just to check in and maintain our relationship. I did everything I could to make sure that when he sold that house, I was the person selling it.

He got a different real estate agent to sell it. Apparently, he caught an episode of *Million Dollar Listing* and thought I was too arrogant on the show, so he went with someone else to teach me a lesson. Some other agent got a commission on what turned out to be a $17 million sale. This guy had made his money selling toys on TV during *X-Men* and *Teenage Mutant Ninja Turtles* cartoons, but somehow he could not understand that the way I'm portrayed on the show may not be a perfect representation of my character. I felt like he hadn't respected the actual work I'd done for him.

So what?

This disappointed me, but I'm not going to let it affect me. I invested a lot of time in my relationship with that guy. His decision doesn't mean I made a bad choice. Not allowing it to affect me is the smartest choice in my industry; maintaining relationships is the best way to get repeat business. And I'm not going to let the reaction of one annoyed cable viewer dissuade me from being on *Million Dollar Listing*. The show has been a huge benefit to my business, and it totally outweighs this one lost commission. So if I've figured out there's no big lesson to take away from this situation, I have to do my best to forget about it and move along. Any more time I spend thinking about it is a waste. My biggest asset in this situation is having a thick skin.

I earned my thick skin the hard way, on a phone. After my brother and I had flipped a few houses, I knew I loved the process, but I didn't think it was going to be my career. I thought of it as a fun, lucrative investment. I was still working for a TV producer and thought my career would be in entertainment. Well, I guess my career is partially in entertainment now. The point is, I didn't realize I'd be turning my focus to real estate.

One of my best friends was renting the guesthouse of the place Matt and I owned and were getting ready to flip. He was kind of a lazy guy I knew from college, and he worked at some mortgage place. He made enough money to pay rent and that was all I cared about.

Then one day he drove up in a Porsche Carrera GT. Clearly something had changed. This guy who was living in my guesthouse had a nicer car than mine. I sat him down in the kitchen and asked him what was going on. He told me that when he started at the mortgage refinance company, he didn't really take the job seriously—calling for two hours, then slacking off. Then a few months ago, he decided to up his game. Now he was there, pounding the phones, from eight A.M. to nine P.M., and it was paying off.

I was very suspicious about how this guy was making all that money. It's LA, so I did have periodic suspicions he might be dealing in some illicit substances. After a few more months passed and the cops never showed up to carry him away, I started to realize this kid might be on to something legit. I took him out to lunch and had him explain everything to me. He took me through the whole sales process, then guaranteed that I would make ten thousand dollars in my first month. I quit my job in TV production. I was going to be a mortgage broker.

This is where the thick skin comes in.

When I went in to interview at the mortgage company, they kept telling me about how great their leads were. They had these awesome leads that were a gold mine of potential sales. On my first day, I sat down at my desk and asked my boss about the leads. He went into his office, came back, and slammed the phone book down on my desk.

"There are your leads."

That was it. There were no secret shortcuts. I was just going to have to call every human being in Los Angeles and see which ones needed to refinance their mortgages. So I did.

Most people don't want to have their dinner interrupted to have some random person talk to them about their mortgage. I had to crawl through a bunch of rejection before I ever found anyone who would even let me make my pitch. The first time someone actually let me talk to him, I panicked. I freaked and yelled out for my manager. He took over the call and closed it. For the first couple of weeks, all I did was open up the calls for somebody else to close them, but pretty soon I had the hang of it and was making my own pitches. The secret was remembering that I wasn't calling to annoy these people; I was calling to help them. I might get two dozen annoyed answers in an hour, people irate I was interrupting *Judge Judy* to annoy them, but to that one person who really *did* need to refinance their home, I was a godsend. I was the person there to solve their problems, and solving their problems was going to make me some money. How good it felt to make money while helping somebody who was paying too much for their house more than made up for the annoyed people yelling at me. I started to learn to ignore them. I started to think more about the results I was going to get than the process I had to go through to get there.

It was rough, but it was the best possible education. Every day, all day long, I pounded phones. I saw these young guys around me making what seemed like vast sums of money to me, and I wanted to learn. I made something like twelve thousand dollars in the first month.

I wasn't a great, natural salesman; I just learned not to take no for an answer. Everyone else in LA had these fun, fancy entertainment jobs. We felt like rebels, outcasts, guys making money off pure fight. It made me proud to be a salesman. Sales is really just like hitting on a girl: You start off nervous, but you push through to make contact. You try to get them to open up and talk to you a little bit, and then you try to get the girl's phone number, or the client's social security number, to close the deal. It's not always going to work, it's maybe not even going to work a majority of the time, but closing feels *so* nice in either situation that you just keep trying.

When I get a new employee these days, I always take them into a neighborhood and make them knock on doors. It is the least scientific way to try to find new clients, but it is the backbone of learning to be a salesperson. You have to hit rejection over and over and over again before you can develop a skin thick enough to pull off your first sale. You have to learn exactly how rejection feels so you won't fear it coming.

This isn't just an issue for salespeople. Any activity you care about is going to involve loss and rejection. If you want to be an actor, you're going to have to audition for a lot of roles before you land anything. If you play football, you will lose sometimes. If you're a chef, some people won't like your food. You must learn from your mistakes, but you cannot let your failures dissuade you from pursuing the thing you love.

Let's be clear: a thick skin doesn't mean being entirely insensitive. One of my greatest advantages when selling mortgage refinances was the ability to pay attention to people and understand their problems. It's why I'm better at selling houses than mortgages, because I'm good at seeing the big picture and finding a strategy for fixing it. You don't need that kind of subtlety when you're just trying to get people to redo a mortgage, but when people are deciding where they're going to raise a family, they need more than a salesperson; they need an advisor and a friend.

There was one high-profile celebrity couple—he's a sports journalist; she's a model—and I found their house for them. I worked hard and got them a great house at a good deal in Hancock Park, and since we were around the same age, we hung out. I thought we were friends.

They resold the house a year later for a million dollars more and they didn't use me for the resale. I asked why and the guy told me, "I wasn't really thrilled with you at the end of the sales process. There were some details you didn't get to quick enough." We provide full, high-end service to our clients. We try to anticipate their needs and be there for them in every way. Unfortunately, we overserviced these clients and they became very dependent on us for services that were far outside the responsibilities of a real estate agent. They were treating us like personal assistants, frequently calling to ask us to go to the property to let in the guy who was going to install the security system, complaining about how the contractors poured the driveway, and asking us to go see how much their trees had grown. Finally, I had to establish boundaries about what we would and wouldn't do, and this guy had gotten mad.

So he didn't use me for the next sale. Learning from mistakes is important, but we also have to understand that some failures aren't mistakes. In this situation, I set a boundary for how much Matt and I were willing to do to accommodate this client, and it cost us a future sale. I also have to understand that if I don't set boundaries, that could cost me the time I need to take care of my other, less vocal clients. I will respect and listen to a client's feedback, but I can't let the rejection of not getting a future sale bother me. I need to look at the facts and make the right decision, not worry about licking my wounds.

Having a tough skin doesn't mean ignoring other people and their needs; it means ignoring the distractions of your emotions. You need to focus on pursuing your goals. Problems, failures, and difficulties may mean you need to reevaluate how you're pursuing those goals, but you can't focus on your own pain or let fear of future pain stop you from moving forward.

Before I worked in mortgages, I was the assistant to a TV producer. If you've ever seen *Entourage* or the movie *Swimming with Sharks,* you kind of understand what it's like to be a Hollywood assistant. These are jobs where tradition requires your boss to be a complete dick to you, and my boss wasn't one to break with tradition. He yelled at me. He gave me stupid, irrelevant tasks. He was constantly telling me how stupid and useless I was. It was like pledging a fraternity, but I didn't get any booze or girls out of the deal. Each day, every day, he made my life a living hell. My job was to ignore the hell and get done what needed to get done. I'm not saying I ignored the lame jobs he gave me; I just tried to ignore all the negativity and insults he decided to couch every comment in. The point of that job is to take all the insults and criticisms and keep going so that one day you can get the better, fancier job and become the person doing the insulting. That isn't the world for me, but I now understand how agents and producers become the deal-making bruisers that run Hollywood. They have to have clear minds when people are yelling at them, celebrities are walking off the set, and millions of dollars are on the line, and the training ground where they learn those skills is getting yelled at because they brought their boss a Diet Coke instead of a Coke Zero.

Years later, I was at Dan Tana's, this famous Italian restaurant on the border of Beverly Hills and West Hollywood where you always see old-school celebrities. My former boss was there, and I'd always vowed that if I saw him, I would either punch him and tell him off or I'd pay for his dinner and tell him off.

I went over and said hello and was nice.

This is Hollywood. At the highest echelons, it's a very small town. If I'd done something cruel or vindictive, people would've heard about it and it would've negatively reflected on me and my business. That doesn't help me in any way. Having a tough skin is the ability to say I won't let my former boss's negativity affect me. I won't let the idea of vengeance against him potentially injure my reputation, because all the yelling he ever did at me didn't really affect me.

And who knows? He will probably need to buy a house one day.

Car accidents, baseball bats, and cancer can hurt you. Words, whether they're insults or rejections, are yours to interpret. You can think of them as an injury, and you can let that affect your future behavior, or you can take them as a challenge. When my former boss told me I was useless, I took it as a challenge to prove my worth. I did, but not to him, to the only person who matters: me. When people reject me, when I tried to pitch them a mortgage refinance or when I try to sell people a house today, I could take it as an insult. I could think it reflects negatively on my skills. Or I could use it as a challenge to make me even hungrier for the next sale.

At the end of the day, having a tough skin fundamentally just means being strong enough to decide what the messages you're being sent mean. I know that I'm smart, capable, and good at my job, so I'm always going to see those messages as challenges, not insults.

Insults and rejection aren't the problem. The problem is that you fear you do not have it in you to be great. Each little rejection is a reminder of your self-doubt. Calculated confidence is going to be impossible as long as you let that doubt rule your decisions. We all have doubt. It is the worst, most negative part of our gut instincts. You just have to recognize it for what it is and ignore it, so that your instincts will be based on what you want and not what you fear. You are stronger than your fear, and that's going to enable you to do amazing things.

Part Two

Fire

Your life right now is fine. You're alive; your country isn't going to get invaded by aliens tomorrow; you probably have food, a house, your health. You may not have one of those things, but if you have even *most* of those things, you're in a better situation than a lot of people in this world.

But you want more than "fine." That's why you're reading this book. You're seeking bigger possibilities from your life. That's going to require more than just hope and good intentions; that's going to require you go out and make some waves. If you want your life to keep evolving, you're going to need to take some risks, make some changes, and be bold. Don't worry. It's really fun.

Every day when I leave my house, I know it's going to be an adventure. I know stuff is going to go wrong, opportunities are going to be presented, and I'm going to have to make thousands of big and small decisions. I can't approach this stuff with uncertainty. I have to be confident—a one-man, problem-solving, decision-making machine. I have to always remember that I'm only a success because of the opportunities I've been able to find in unlikely places, and I have to keep looking for them. I have to be on fire and ready to fire all day long.

It makes my life better.

In this part of the book, I'm going to tell you how to use these techniques to succeed and how having the confidence necessary to fire will help you achieve your goals. But right now, let me take a moment out to say that it doesn't just make your life better because of the results it will bring, but also because it will fill your life with purpose. Making sales makes me happy, yes, but spending a whole day *on,* feeling like I'm being exactly the kind of man, fiancé, and real estate agent I want to be, makes me feel amazing. It makes me feel like I'm not wasting a single moment of my life, and nothing's more valuable than that.

You can be the person who's always ready to fire. If you train your gut to trust your smartest instincts and ignore your irrational fears, you're going to be ready to make quick decisions and see them pay off.

The key is execution. This part of the book is primarily about establishing the habits that will turn you into a deal maker. Confidence requires more than instincts and decisions; it requires believing in yourself enough to get your plans moving and to stick with them until they are complete. It's hard. Self-doubt is always waiting to sabotage you, but if you can ignore it and focus on your goals, the rewards are innumerable.

You don't get better at things by thinking about them; you get better by doing. Whatever you want out of life—to be rich, to have a successful marriage, to have the best damned tomatoes in any vegetable garden in the state—the only way to start learning what you need to know is by doing it. You can read all the books and talk to all the people, but you're not going to learn the lessons that *you* need to learn about something until you start doing it. The best part is you're going to get to do something you love in the process.

I'm not saying you're going to be perfect from the start—far from it. I'm just saying that a strong habit of *doing* is going to put you in the strongest possible position to succeed eventually. Action will always beat inaction.

You're the CEO of your own life. Stop acting like an employee. Develop a strategy, and get out there and start executing it. In the words of the great poet Eminem, "You only get one shot, do not miss your chance to blow."

8

Get in the Game

Being perfect is not about that scoreboard out there. . . . Being perfect is about being able to look your friends in the eye and know that you didn't let them down because you told them the truth. And that truth is that you did everything that you could. There wasn't one more thing that you could've done.

—Coach Gary Gaines (played by Billy Bob Thornton), *Friday Night Lights* (based on the book by Buzz Bissinger)

You don't win unless you try. We all know that, but we all manage to avoid trying on a regular basis. Trying is scary. It's giving the world the opportunity to tell you that you're not nearly as talented as you hoped you were. Trying is the first step in failing, but if you can't face that fact and take the risk anyway, you're never going to do anything with your life.

Getting in the game is putting your talents on the line. It is risking rejection and failure so you can also have the chance of earning respect and reward. You're never going to put out all the effort, all the focus, all the desire, to be a success unless that risk of failure is there. You only live once. This is the only game you're ever going to play. You need to leave everything you have on that field.

Like I said earlier, I played football in college. It was awesome. Syracuse University had a powerhouse program, I got to feel like a big deal on campus, and I played with future pros like Donovan McNabb. I should have loved it more than I did, but there was a problem. I was a kicker.

See, a football team is a hundred guys, gigantic mountains of men, who go out and sweat and scrape and battle for hours. And four guys in nice clean uniforms who go out and kick the ball two or three times during a game. It killed me to watch my friends digging deep, giving their lives to turn the tide in a game, while I sat on the bench waiting.

I played football in high school and college because this is America and football gets you attention, respect, and scholarships, but my heart always belonged to soccer because that was a game where I could be in the mix the whole time. In soccer, everyone's a kicker; in football, I was a one-trick pony.

Syracuse had a great team while I was there, and we made it to the Orange Bowl and the Fiesta Bowl while I was playing. I still remember the thrill of running out of that tunnel and onto the field as 80,000 people in the stadium were roaring in anticipation for the game. The feeling of sitting next to that game, however, knowing I'd probably never play a single down, was the worst. I got all the benefit of being a Syracuse football player with almost none of the risk, but that wasn't a good thing. I needed to feel like my hard work was helping the team I was on. I needed to get in the game.

So I quit football. I knew that I needed a game where I could be there, in the game, being the guy who's making the plays that win or lose the game. That's been true of my professional life too. I've had a lot of fun, interesting jobs, but I could never really fall in love with a job that didn't let me be the person in the driver's seat. Working in mail rooms and as a producer's assistant were great jobs that many people would have killed to land, but I needed a job where I could connect my foot with the ball on a regular basis.

And let's not pretend like the only problem was the jobs. When I graduated from college, I didn't really know what I wanted. I wasn't completely ready to get in the game professionally. When I got that job selling phone service to businesses, I saw it as a way to earn money to have fun at night and on the weekends. It wasn't a perfect fit for me, but let's be honest. I was lazy. I didn't know the product, I didn't know the competition, and I didn't have a strategy. You can't really be a great salesman unless you know all that stuff. I wasn't *really* in the game, so I was never going to be a success at it.

So what I'm saying is that the only way you can really succeed is to take on challenges. With that first condo my brother and I bought, I risked my own money on something I really loved, and I rose to the occasion. It's not as clean or simple as managing stocks, but it's what gets my blood going. I took a risk and it felt good.

The digging deep hasn't gone away either. I had this client who built a house in Beverly Hills that I sold for $7 million. The buyers were some crazy-rich Chinese guys I'd never met until they came for a walk-through when we were in escrow. After one look at the place, they said they were cancelling the deal. The house wasn't ready. It was a beautiful, modern place in the flats of Beverly Hills, but there was paint on the windows and ripped screens. The developer I represented thought he had his deal. "It's too late. They already lifted contingencies." He wasn't going to do anything further to make this deal happen. The buyers were working through a real estate agent who didn't really know LA real estate and barely spoke English. It was a deal about to crash, and it seemed like the developer I was working with was just as happy to sue the buyers for breach of contract as he was to sell the house.

I had a situation on my hands that was about to implode into two annoyed clients and a year or more of litigation. I didn't aim. I fired. I went out and hired my own contractor with my own money to finish the house the way it should have been finished.

Why spend my money on this house when I'm under no obligation to do so? Because this is my business. I had two wealthy clients who weren't going to back down and were perfectly willing to involve each other and me in an endless court case. I could take $20,000 of a $180,000 commission and fix the problem, make both sides happy, and preserve my reputation as someone who closes deals cleanly and amicably. I've decided that I'm going to be a guy who's business is making clients happy, so I'm sure as hell going to do what it takes to get the job done. That's what getting in the game is about.

If you're going to be in business, it's your job to get the business done. Explaining why you can't be blamed for something or listening to people tell you why you can't do it are great ways of avoiding ever doing anything significant with your life. Intelligent risks are what built all of human society, and they can make you really rich.

Let's talk about Eric Edelson. In August of 2008 he was a Stanford MBA graduate in between consulting jobs. He got a call from a friend's dad, Mike Looney, who had partnered with a local tile expert, Paul Burns, to produce an ecologically friendly countertop material called BottleStone. The guys wanted Eric's help putting together a business plan to enter a competition for innovative building materials. Eric didn't have anything better to do and needed to make some money, so he said he'd help.

But 2008 was the year the subprime mortgage bubble burst, Lehman Brothers went bankrupt, and the Great Recession began. Home construction was hit pretty hard, and Paul Burns's company, Fireclay Tile, was in dire straits. In January 2009 Eric told Looney and Burns that developing Bottle-Stone was going to be more expensive than they'd previously thought, but by this point, Burns wasn't worried about eco-friendly tile; he was worried about his business going under. He asked Eric for advice.

Burns was in no position to pay him, but Eric was pretty certain he could spend a week investigating the company and come back with a strong plan. He found the kind of informal business practices that are common in family businesses, but he also saw a strong, clear path for this company to keep going.

When Eric presented his findings to Burns, however, Burns admitted he didn't have the skills or knowledge to implement them. He knew tile, not business.

Eric was frustrated. He was ready to go off to a lucrative job as an executive at a large company, where he'd offer advice, assemble presentations, and never really have to take a major risk, but he knew his plan for Fireclay Tile could work. Maybe Eric could implement the plan.

Eric took over as CEO of Fireclay. He knew it would mean low pay and risky prospects, but he also knew that the soul of business isn't spreadsheets and PowerPoints. It's making good products and selling them to the people who need them.

Since Eric took over, Fireclay has repositioned its brand as a provider of tile handmade in California from recycled materials. The company maintained viability in a depressed market by emphasizing its sustainable manufacturing processes and, through that, has built relationships with environmentally conscious businesses like Google, Whole Foods, and Starbucks.[15]

Eric didn't just get to give someone else the plan to succeed this time; he got to be the success, because he put his knowledge of business on the line and took a risk. It could have gone badly. All the business savvy in the world cannot save some businesses, especially an American manufacturer of building materials in 2008 and 2009. But if Fireclay Tile hadn't survived, Eric still would have gotten a better, stronger understanding of business than any of his MBA classmates who've never left a boardroom. Winning is definitely better than losing, but if you don't play, that's just boring.

What're your goals? You like a guy? Ask him out. You'd like to maybe start a handbag line? Get some leather and some scissors, and see where they take you. You want to save a struggling tile company, scrap your career plans, and take it over? Well, that may not be an option for everyone. I'm not saying you should be stupid with your resources. I'm saying activity is always better than inactivity.

Yeah, you could ask that guy out and have him say no. You could make a bad handbag. You could spend six months running a tile manufacturer just to have it go bankrupt. Failure doesn't go away, but it also doesn't kill you. Once you've started doing, once you've gotten in the game, you're going to be learning and growing, and most important, you're going to be thinking of yourself as a player.

The mind-set of a player is key. The right mind-set turns your goals into a set of habits. Let's look at that Beverly Hills house deal again: My decision to pay for a construction crew wasn't based on a single outcome. My primary concern wasn't with a single outcome. I wasn't motivated by wanting my commission. My decision was based on the way I see myself. I am a real estate agent. I close deals. I am a player.

Whether I'm winning or losing, I get the satisfaction of knowing I'm going out there every day and leaving everything I've got on the playing field. Sure, maybe no one else is looking at it as a game, but they shouldn't be. For most of my clients, this is a process they'll go through three or four times in their lives. They're finding the right place to let their family grow or getting rid of Mom's house as one of the steps of finalizing her estate. But I'm a real estate agent. They're paying me to know how this process works, so I better be living, loving, and learning from every moment I get to be involved in this process.

Being a player is the first step in becoming a pro. Engaging in the stuff you love will teach you valuable lessons that you can keep applying. The fear of failure is what may keep you from trying in the first place, but it is only the repeated act of doing that will earn you the skills you need to be amazing. You're scared to try because you know there are people who are better, but trying, a lot of trying, is what will allow you to be one of those people. I want to be a pro, so I will do what it takes to play, even if it costs me.

Today I was on the phone with a developer client. He was offering $2.95 million on a place; the sellers were standing firm at $3 million. I said I'd kick in $25,000 of my commission if I could get the other agent to do the same. He asked why I'd do that. The simple answer is that it still leaves me with fifty grand. The bigger answer is because I'm a real estate agent. I close deals. I'm more concerned with making sure good deals close than I am with squeezing every penny out of every deal. That's because I think being in good shape, being practiced, experienced, and familiar with my business, is way more important than any single deal.

Do it, move on, and keep doing it. That is a recipe for success. Any time you spend wondering if trying is a good idea is just wasted time. If you think you might want to be a singer, go to an open mic night. If it was hard, if you embarrassed yourself, if your voice cracked, go do it again. You'll be better, you'll be more relaxed, and you'll be even better the third time. If it's something you truly love, that process won't just make you better; it'll also let you have a lot of fun.

Calculated confidence isn't a skill you can learn in a classroom; it's a life skill. It's something that can only be shaped by challenging yourself to make hard decisions quickly, then learn from your results. Getting good at reading situations and reacting to them is an ongoing process of honing your instincts to better evaluate and respond to problems. You won't always be good at it, but the more you keep fighting toward your goals and trusting your instincts, the better you'll get.

You have to keep trying. If you choose not to stop, you will be unstoppable.

9

Screw It, You Got to See What Happens

The biggest risk is not taking any risk. . . .
In a world that's changing really quickly,
the only strategy that is guaranteed
to fail is not taking any risks.

—Mark Zuckerberg

Simple choices make for simple lives. Every day we make easy, comfortable choices that give us predictable results. That's a good thing. Lives full of chaos only make sense in movies and the Real Housewives franchise. What's important is that we don't get so stuck in the ruts of what's comfortable that we're not able to make the big, daring choices that are required to elevate our lives out of normalcy. Boring choices may keep you safe and content, but they won't make you rich, successful, or, in my opinion, truly happy.

You decide what genre of movie your life is going to be. Is it going to be a romantic comedy, a tragedy, or a very boring documentary about what it's like to be a shoe salesman in Toledo, Ohio. (Not that there's anything wrong with shoe salesmen. That's how my grandfather got his start!) I have decided that my life is going to be an adventure, so I'm going to have to take on some (calculated) challenges to keep things interesting.

That isn't just a plan for a more interesting life; it is building the skills for success.

New challenges are scary—the vague, irrational scary of the unknown. The fear of the unknown is one of the worst instincts we have, and one we must train ourselves to ignore. In key situations, when you have opportunities that could change your life, that fear will tempt you to be risk averse and to make the simple, easy, boring choice. When you push yourself out of your comfort zone in any aspect of your life, you are training yourself to be able to ignore your irrational fears and trust the messages your mind and your better instincts are giving you. That's the core of calculated confidence.

I read about a study where professors ran some hypothetical investments past different groups of people with different approaches to risk: rock climbers, smokers, race car drivers, and a student control group. They tried to figure out if the people who sought risk in their regular lives would tend to be riskier investors. The results were surprising: The race car drivers were far and away the most rational investors. They weren't taking risks for their own sake, but they were more capable of ignoring low-probability risks.[16]

Think about it. Race car drivers spend every day doing a job with a very small chance of very big danger. They have to focus themselves on what they can control and not let low-probability dangers get in the way of keeping all their attention on the high-precision driving they need to be doing. So race car drivers, by regularly dealing with risky situations, train themselves to intellectually know that the risks exist but to not let them affect their decision making. They know the dangers exist, but they work to not fear them.

Sometimes you gotta see what happens. What I'm saying is, one time I did mushrooms.

Now, let me be clear. I've never really been a drug user. When I was a kid, I was a *huge* Boston Celtics fan. They were my life, and when they got to the second pick of the first round of the 1986 NBA draft, I was so excited. They snagged Len Bias, a gigantic forward from the University of Maryland, who immediately became my hero. Two days later, Len celebrated by doing some cocaine, overdosed, and died.

Drugs like cocaine and heroin are a real risk and I've avoided them my entire life. But . . . in my junior year of college one of my frat brothers came around the house saying he had mushrooms. I knew they weren't addictive, I was surrounded by all my friends, and I had never really seen an after-school special about someone throwing themselves out of a window because they did mushrooms. Based on what friends had told me about mushrooms, I figured this was not a major-risk situation. I couldn't logically think of a strong reason not to do it, so I told myself, *Screw it, you gotta see what happens.*

Well it turns out that before you see what happens, you have to taste what happens. That mushroom was *gross.* I had to make a peanut butter sandwich and put the 'shroom in it so I could choke it down.

And then the journey began. I walked around the house and things started to feel a little funny. I noticed a mask—like from that movie *Eyes Wide Shut*—on the ground. I put the mask on and it *became part of my face*. A while later, everything turned blue. Like, I could still see and distinguish between objects, but they were all blue. It was an amazing experience. I've tried it and I never need to do it again, but I'm glad that in the moment I was able to have the courage to do something outside of my comfort zone.

We're all trained to be scared of making quick, resolute decisions. We're constantly supposed to be worried about some intangible unknown, and that's what makes us slow and full of doubt. I want you to ask yourself what this constant level of doubt gets you. Has there ever been a situation where your reticence saved you? Or have you spent your life talking yourself out of opportunities for fun, profit, and adventure?

Sometimes—not all the time—you have to just go with a hunch. If your gut gives you a solid tug in a direction and you can't see any obvious problems, go for it. The tiny problems you might end up fretting about are exactly the stuff that those professional race car drivers have taught themselves to ignore. You can too. The only difference is that the race car you're driving is your career.

———

'm not just a real estate agent; I'm also a real estate investor. I'm always on the lookout for a great property to put my own money into. Last year I was presented with one of these "screw it" moments. I was checking out the MLS, like you know I love to do. (I am on that thing every day, constantly hitting refresh. The way most people screw around on Facebook, I can't stop checking the MLS. Think about that. What if you spent all the time you spend on Facebook doing something that could get you ahead and make you money? Who cares what your ex-boyfriend is doing; think about what you're doing. The MLS is my religion.)

Usually, the MLS has just the same houses that have been sitting on the market for three years, but on this day, a new house popped up. Its location was ridiculous, sitting just half a block up the hill from the Sunset Strip in West Hollywood. If the most important thing in real estate is location, then whatever this place looked like, it was a gem. I couldn't believe something like this had hit the market without me knowing anything about it.

They were asking $3 million. Anywhere else, that's a lot of money for a lot of house, but in this location, with a 25,000-square-foot lot, it's nothing. It meant the place was a teardown. In LA real estate if a house isn't amazing but it's in a great location, its value is primarily in its plot of land. This looked like it might be exactly the kind of house a person could buy and tear down, then build a new house on the property worth five to ten times the original price. I had hit gold.

The listing agent was a name I didn't know. The company he worked for was in South LA, so I knew I would be dealing with someone who was relatively unfamiliar with Hollywood Hills real estate. I knew there was potentially a very good deal at hand. I called immediately. He was in the house when he answered. The owner had died recently and the real estate agent was there, setting the house in order to get it ready for a sale. I told him I was a neighbor and asked if I could come over. He said he was getting ready to leave. I said I could be there in seven minutes.

This was a Thursday. The first day he could possibly show it would be Tuesday. If I let that house be shown to the public, every real estate agent and developer in West Hollywood and Beverly Hills would be all over it, making offers. I needed to hit quickly.

The first thing I saw was a gate. This place was completely hidden from the street. A super-long driveway took me up to the house. In the Hollywood Hills, privacy usually means having to drive thirty minutes up winding roads. A place with this level of seclusion that close to the Strip was something special.

And at the same time, the house was terrible. Like 1966 had exploded, then turned into a house: pinks, purples, popcorn ceilings, and of course the accumulated tchotchkes of a grandma who'd lived a long and happy life. I didn't know that many ceramic elephants existed in the world, let alone in a single house.

It was a great location and a not-so-great house. It would take vision, but someone could really make money off this place. I knew *nothing* about this place except the location, the asking price, and what it looked like, but what else is there to know? I was playing with my own money this time, not somebody else's, so I had the liberty I needed to take a risk. If I let somebody else snag this place, I'd be kicking myself for years. And I knew *exactly* what this place was worth. I'd sold the lot five houses down—a much smaller, much less impressive lot—

six months before for $2.3 million. Before I had time to think, my gut was telling me to make an offer on the place.

Fuck it, I said to myself. *You gotta see what happens.* I had been there less than ten minutes when I made my offer.

He was asking for $3 million. I offered $2.2 million. The real estate agent wasn't anywhere near ready to deal with a negotiation, so I did the thing no real estate agent is supposed to do: I negotiated against myself. I raised the offer to $2.3. He bit. He could cut out all the work and uncertainty of listing a house and he and his clients would walk away with almost what they were asking. I emailed my assistant. She put together the offer, sent it to the real estate agent, and he went to ask his clients if they were okay with the offer.

They agreed, and the place was mine.

Oh shit. Did I make a horrible mistake?

A couple of days later, the agent called me to tell me how lucky I was. He'd started getting calls from real estate agents offering to buy the place at or above asking price. Next thing you know, they were calling me. One guy offered me $350,000 just to take over my contract. It was becoming clear that I hadn't made a mistake. In fact, trusting my instincts had allowed me to make the quick decisions necessary to secure that house before anyone else had a chance to make an offer.

I had no clue what I was going to do with that place. Should I sell it? Move in and renovate it? Package it with permits and plans for a tear-down? In the months after I bought the place, I didn't have nearly as much clarity as I'd had in those moments in the house. Now I had lots of options and the time to talk myself out of all of them. Eventually, I just had to let myself make a choice. Everything comes with risks and costs. You just have to know that they're there and take them, because they're the only way you ever get a payoff. I sold that house six months later and profited more than $1 million.

Playing by the rules is likely to get you a pretty boring life. Ignoring all the rules is likely to get you ten to twenty years in a federal prison. You have to be smart, but cautious isn't the same as smart. When you're presented with an opportunity and your gut instinct is to say no, you need to inventory what the real, concrete risks are, what the likelihood of them happening is, and how possible it is that there are dangers you're not educated enough to identify. If you do that and you still don't have a good solid reason not to do it, you're probably just responding to fear of the unknown. I'm not saying you should take a chance every time, or even most times, but sometimes you should do it. It's fun, and it teaches you a lot about yourself.

Your irrational fear is of hidden risks. Those do exist. Every birthday present you open might contain a snake, but they probably don't. Every dark hole in the woods might contain a snake. Again, they probably don't, but the likelihood of a snake being present is higher in the woods. You have to use your intellect to judge which risks are reasonable and which are stupid. Fear is one of those instincts you have to keep in check in your brain, because the new horizons it's trying to keep you from exploring are pretty great.

One of the best examples of a business ignoring the risks of new territory is also the most famous. In the late '90s, British shoe manufacturer W. J. Brooks, Ltd., was faltering due to competition from cheaper imported men's dress shoes. One day a woman from a sex shop called the owner, Steve Pateman, to ask him if he had women's shoes in men's sizes. He didn't, but he told her he could make them. Steve kept his business afloat by making shoes for drag queens, cross-dressers, and transgender people, and the business inspired the movie *Kinky Boots,* which then inspired a Broadway musical.

A few years later, Steve's business went under. After the movie made other shoe manufacturers realize that high heels for men was an untapped market, they started moving in and Steve was again faced with competition from cheaper imports. Steve's risk had kept the company alive for a few more years, but it didn't fix everything. I'm not saying every big decision will save your factory or make you rich; I'm saying big decisions will be more interesting than safe decisions. Nobody wants to watch a movie called *Safe Decisions* (and if they did, I'm sure a musical based on it would suck).

Stop fearing the unknown. You can and should fear stuff you concretely know is dangerous, but if your aversion to a new opportunity is based exclusively on an irrational fear, that may just be primal, animal instinct. The only way you can learn about new ideas and experiences is to go exploring. Use your best judgment, but let your brain make the decisions. Risky, novel decisions won't always turn out the way you hope, but they also won't be the realization of your worst fears. If something feels like an opportunity, take it. If you spend too much time worrying about hidden risks, you may find out that your opportunity is now somebody else's success story.

10

Always Have a House to Show

Be prepared.

—Boy Scout motto

One day, at the beginning of my career, I was driving around with a hard-working agent who worked down in the flats of Beverly Hills. We pulled up to an open house and a potential buyer was walking out. The agent knew him and said, "Hi." They chatted, discussed some listings, and then my agent friend said, "I have the perfect house to show you. You should come by and see it tomorrow." They set up the appointment and we drove off.

I asked the agent which house he was going to show this buyer. He said, "I don't know yet. I'll go back to the office and figure out the best one to show him. Always have a house to show."

That's the most basic truth, and nobody understands it. It's not just a real estate thing. Whatever you do, whatever contacts or opportunities are presented to you, be ready to pursue them *now*. You meet a cute girl, have a barbecue to take her to. Someone tells you that they like your spec screenplay, have a pitch to show them. If you wait for the perfect house or pitch or barbecue, the contact is going to be forgotten. If you start pursuing it now, at least you'll be building a relationship. You have to strike while you're fresh in their mind. If you wait, they'll move along to something new.

The thing is, I usually have the perfect house for someone. When I meet a person on the street, I may not know exactly which house it is, but if I go through my listings, one of my houses is going to be a pretty spot-on fit for that person. Well, for anybody who's actually in the market for a house in the Hollywood Hills.

When I meet someone, I may not be able to say where the house is or what it looks like, but I have enough professional respect for myself to know I've got a diverse and high-quality portfolio of houses to choose from in any situation. If you're pursuing a career, you give a lot of yourself to it. Have some respect for the work you've done and believe that it's good. Don't wait for your album to be perfect; wait until you have the opportunity to share it with your clients, then let them know you have something they will *love*.

A few months ago, I got a call from a guy who said his boss wanted to look at a place I represented. He said his boss didn't like using real estate agents, so he would just call the listing agents directly. I was impressed by the balls on this guy, so I set up an appointment. It wasn't until he showed up that I realized the boss in question was a major film producer, who was married to a very famous model. Let's call them Mr. Big and Ms. Legs.

Matt and I showed them the house. They loved it, and fifteen days later, we were in escrow on the house. Things were going *great* . . . until we found a lien on the house they were trying to buy. The lien basically made it impossible for them to get clean title to the house. The deal was dead.

So I told Mr. Big I had the perfect house to show him. This wasn't just a business tactic. Mr. Big is a business mogul. He'd see right through anyone who was trying to sell him a bill of goods. I just knew that I was one of the very few people who could satisfy the needs of such a high-end couple, so I was willing to put everything on the line to keep them as clients.

I did have the perfect house. It wasn't just a house; it was on the site of the former Errol Flynn estate: $7.9 million, one acre in the Hollywood Hills. It wasn't the original Errol Flynn house, which got torn down to make way for something more modern in the '90s. This was an A-list movie star property, and it was perfect for Mr. Big. I had it, and I was ready to show it.

He didn't buy it. Turns out it wasn't perfect enough. What matters is that I never let the relationship rest. I was always working to build it, and Mr. Big was impressed. His manager called to let us know that Ms. Legs was selling her house and they wanted us to represent it. You have to be a Boy Scout (always prepared) and a rock star (always exceeding people's expectations) if you want to turn every opportunity into a profitable business relationship.

I've got this one client I've sold six houses to. He's not a developer; he's just got a different approach to home ownership than most people. I've been able to turn that approach into a very profitable relationship for both of us because I've always had a house to show him.

I had repped this guy who was a New Yorker and who was always looking for a house in LA but never actually bought one. He had made me no money, but he did tell his friend about me. The friend had made a bunch of money as a talent agent for Hollywood folks. He's been doing this for a long time, he's very smart, and damn, he likes to close a deal.

The dude called me up as I was walking out of an open house. He told me what he was looking for, and I told him I had the perfect house. I'd seen it twenty minutes before and the listing agents had told me they were getting ready to drop it from $6.3 million to $5.5. It hadn't been changed in the listings yet; this was just a little bit of information they'd tossed my way because I was such a charming guy.

And I needed to toss that tidbit somebody else's way if I wanted to make any money off it. I told him about the price reduction and said we could maybe get them even lower.

He bought it for $4.3 million. We sold it a year and a half later for $6.2 million.

So, like I said, this guy isn't a developer; he doesn't flip houses. He's just a wealthy former talent agent with good taste, a great art collection, and a willingness to sell his house at any point in time. He moves into these places, he puts up his art, and the house looks a million times better because of the high-end furnishings. Almost as soon as he's in the place, he's ready to start showing it to buyers to see if he can make some money.

How has he been so successful? Because he really has calculated confidence. This guy has enough money to *close*. He can walk in and tell you that he can write a check today for $4.3 million. He opened escrow the day after I showed him the house and closed three days later. No banks involved, no waiting. He's got the liquid cash. If he can smell the desperation on anyone, he'll strike, offering them the cool certainty that money's coming if they'll just shave—oh, I don't know—$2 million off their original asking price.

I'm not just suggesting you tell everyone that you have the perfect house or barbecue or pitch for them. I'm saying you should *be* the kind of person who does have that perfect thing. Every Tuesday I go to see twelve new houses. Most agents go to look at one cool house. I need to know that I know everything about the products in my market so I can say with confidence "This is the best deal for you" or "There's no better view in Beverly Hills."

So I kept in contact with this talent agent guy and eventually said, "Hey, this place looks great. We should try to sell it." Like I said, he made almost a $2 million profit. We flipped him into another house. He sold that one a week later for a $1 million profit.

Sometimes I wonder if this guy is a genie or something.

The second house had belonged to an infomercial fitness guru. It was a great house in a great location in the hills, but the style was a very dark, orangey Mediterranean that doesn't sell that well. The house sat on the market for years, with the price slowly reducing over time. A magical thing happens when a house actually hits the price it should be: people come out of the woodwork to buy it. So as my client was in escrow on this place, some people who'd been looking at it got so pissed off someone had snagged the home they wanted that they offered to pay an additional $1 million to take over my client's contract.

He never moved in and made a million dollars off it.

I've sold this guy six houses, and I'm going to sell him more, because every time he seems interested in doing some business in real estate, I have somewhere to take him.

You also have to be prepared to prove yourself when you've got the opportunity.

In the '90s, Peter Dragone and John Sylvan had an idea for a coffeemaker that could efficiently make one cup of coffee at a time. Sylvan had worked at a semiconductor company where it seemed impossible for his coworkers to successfully operate the coffeemaker, so he had dreamed of a world where each time he went for some coffee, one properly made cup could be his quickly.

The guys spent years in Sylvan's condo, building machines that used too little pressure, which didn't get any coffee out of the machine, or too much pressure, which sent coffee grounds and scalding water flying all over his kitchen. The biggest challenge, though, was making the small pods of coffee grounds. The guys would cut filter paper cones, insert them into plastic cups, add the coffee grounds, then use a clothes iron to seal the tops. It was an excruciatingly slow, messy process.

In the mid '90s, they finally had the technology ready to show to investors, but Sylvan realized he couldn't properly show off the ease and efficiency of the machine without blowing through a bunch of coffee pods in a single demonstration. He could just use one or two and try to get the investors to understand how easy the process would be once the pods were mass produced, but he realized that would be a mistake. The only way to make investors understand was to make it feel like the pods were already being mass produced.

He hired temp labor and taught them how to make the pods. After a few weeks of his house full of temps playing arts and crafts, he was ready to start showing the machine to investors. One asked how much the coffee pods cost, and Sylvan smiled and said, "Fifty bucks." Both men laughed. Only Sylvan knew how close to true the number was, but he also knew that expense meant he'd never be in a situation where he wouldn't have a cup of coffee to show off.

Or so they thought. Dragone and Sylvan packed up a machine and some of the pods to show to a Minnesota-based investor. When they got to their hotel, they opened up their box of samples and discovered that the air pressure changes in the cargo hold of their flight had caused all the pods to explode. They knew they couldn't pitch without having samples, so the guys stayed up all night with the hotel's complimentary iron, meticulously repacking their coffee pods.

The investor, Food Fund, gave Dragone and Sylvan's company, Keurig, it's first investment of fifty thousand dollars, and later that year Dragone and Sylvan got a million more. Now 13 percent of all coffee machines sold in the United States are

Keurigs. Those coffee pods the guys threw together in the hotel room may not have been perfect, but they were good enough.[17]

We are always looking for those great opportunities that will give us a chance to prove ourselves, but when the time comes, we are all too likely to shy away from acting on them. We want to have the perfect thing to say, the perfect sample to show, the perfect house. Don't wait for perfect, go with the best that you have. That's far more likely to build on your opportunity than nothing at all.

Let's take another example from outside of real estate. You know who Vin Diesel is, right? The huge star of blockbusters like The Fast and the Furious franchise? Well, back in the '90s he didn't have much of a movie career. Casting directors really didn't know what to do with a ripped half-Italian, half-black guy. He didn't easily fit into any of the roles they were casting, so he never booked anything, so he didn't have anything to show anyone who might be interested in him.

So Vin Diesel made a house to show.

Well, it wasn't a house; it was a short film. He also made it the *perfect* short film to show people it was the story of a yoked half-Italian, half-black actor who never booked parts because he didn't easily fit into the parts that were being cast. And most important, it was good. Steven Spielberg saw Vin's movie *Multi-Facial,* learned that Vin did good work but was having trouble booking roles, and designed a part in *Saving Private Ryan* for him. That is a success story.

The minute you meet someone, you're telling a story of who you are and what you do. Having a house to show is about taking an immediate, active role in shaping that story. If someone expresses interest in buying or selling a house, I need to immediately let them know I'm in real estate and I do good work. But I can't just tell somebody that I do good work; I have to show them.

I could wait for more perfect houses for any of my clients. Vin Diesel could have waited until he got his first big movie break before trying to sell himself. Instead, he used his own time, talent, and four thousand dollars and made his first big movie break, then leveraged that into the kind of role every young actor dreams of.

You may be scared you're not good at what you do. If you're someone who works hard and smart, that's probably an unreasonable, unfounded fear, but you may use that fear to avoid taking risks. You may be scared the professional you are isn't up to the challenge of achieving real success, so you have to wait around for some other, better you with other, better work samples to show up before you make the push for big success. That other you isn't coming. You have to become her or him. Stop waiting to be more prepared. Just take the risk and put yourself out there.

It's only through work that you grow. Not school or training or work in the abstract; you grow through real-world work. You grow by showing houses, selling the best you've got, and learning from the mistakes you make along the way.

I'm on TV, my suits are sharp, and my lady is very, very beautiful. If I wanted to hide behind my persona, I could, but that would be the beginning of the end for real success in my life. I've already said that life is a game so you should get in the game and play it. I've already said that fearing risk turns you into a boring and mediocre person. Always having a house to show is practicing all these ideas. It's turning challenging yourself into a habit. If "Screw it, you got to see what happens" is about saying yes to unusual possibilities when they present themselves, "Always have a house to show" is about maximizing those usual possibilities. Opportunities die around you every day. Don't lose out. Become the kind of person who's ready to find success everywhere.

There's no use waiting for a better you to come around. Trust that the skills and instincts you've built are valuable and that who you are right now is worthy of respect. I know you don't want to screw up a big opportunity, but not pursuing that opportunity is the best way to let it die. Your talents deserve to be recognized, so show them to somebody.

11

Your Gut Is the Godfather, Your Head Is the Consigliere

Sometimes I feel that I am right.
I do not know that I am.

—Albert Einstein, from an interview with
George Sylvester Viereck published in the
Saturday Evening Post, October 26, 1929

Albert Einstein was a smart guy. I don't think I'm really going out on a limb by saying that, so it's always interesting when you see a quote from him that says something like he *feels* that he is right when he doesn't know he's right. Maybe that works when you're arguing with your wife (and maybe that's why Einstein went through two of them), but when it comes to physics, you kind of have to do the math, right?

Clearly, Einstein did the math. He's Einstein, but there's something great about realizing that even *his* process started out from a place of gut instinct. Even in the most abstract, theoretical stuff, your gut can be putting facts together before your brain has a chance to figure out all the details.

Decision making, creativity, and leadership aren't just about intuition; intuition is just a start. Einstein still had to do the math, and you still have to figure out how to pursue the goals you set for yourself. It's like in *The Godfather:* Don Corleone was in charge. He was the godfather, but Tom Hagen (that's Robert Duvall) was the consigliere, the counselor. He's the guy who figured out *how* to get stuff done, who warned the godfather about stuff he hadn't thought about and made sure all the math added up.

Your gut is the godfather. It's giving you the big-picture direction. Your brain is the consigliere. It's there to figure out the strategies to achieve the godfather's goals.

The relationship between intellectual thinking and gut reaction is complex. You always think following rational paths is the best choice, but doing that can allow you to ignore stuff that matters.

In his book *Blink,* Malcolm Gladwell tells the story of an ancient Greek statue that came on the market for $10 million. Experts did analysis for over a year, and everything factually seemed to indicate this was a twenty-five-hundred-year-old statue from the Mediterranean. Then an art historian looked at it and just said, "Nope."

Nope. Federico Zeri just *knew* it wasn't authentic. His decades of experience and learning synthesized into an understanding of his field complete and simple enough to tell that it was a forgery. He didn't have intellectual proof; he had instinct. He was right. The statue was carved by a group of art forgers from Rome. All the research done on the stone samples and the layers of calcite from aging had just reinforced a well-crafted lie. It was a thousand tiny factors together that told the truth.

Lying is actually one of those areas where instinct is more reliable than rational thought. During a study at UC Berkeley, test subjects were shown videos of people lying and telling the truth, then the subjects were given a chance to try to figure out which was which. Their determinations were less accurate than if they had randomly guessed. Then the directors of the study tested people's immediate, gut reactions to the same liars and truth tellers. The gut reactions were *way* more accurate.[18]

Hotel magnate Conrad Hilton had a great story of gut-based business decision making. There was a property being sold through a blind bidding process. Hilton had decided, rationally, that $159,000 was how much the place was worth, and he was ready to bid that amount. Then one morning he woke up with the number $174,000 stuck in his head. He couldn't get rid of it, so he bid that amount for the property. The next highest bid was a thousand dollars less: $173,000. Hilton got the place, he paid the cheapest possible amount for it, and he subsequently sold it for millions of dollars.

But gut instinct can steer you wrong. We all know something about irrational reactions: being afraid of the dark, instantly liking someone who turns out to be a conman, believing *Green Lantern* was going to be a good movie.

One of the best stories of gut instinct telling lies and intellectual analysis cutting through the crap is *Moneyball,* Michael Lewis's awesome recounting of Oakland A's manager Billy Beane and his use of math to change the game of professional baseball.

When Beane took over the Oakland A's, they had a scouting system that, in many ways, relied on the gut instincts of the scouts. The scouts looked at traditional stats, yes, but also at the players who *seemed* like baseball stars—attractive white guys who seemed confident and capable and had cute girlfriends. Beane understood the shortcomings of this system, because he had been one of those golden boys the scouts were clamoring after. He had been a first-round pick in the 1980 MLB draft, received a $125,000 signing bonus, and then failed to distinguish himself as a player in any way. After four years in the minors and a few abortive trips up to the major leagues, he was done as a baseball player.

Beane realized the shortcomings of this intuition-based system, and he used logic and a lot of math to break through it. Baseball stats geeks had come up with a system called "sabermetrics," which analyzed the numbers, and Beane figured out that it wasn't flashy stuff like home runs that won baseball games; it was players who got on base. Nothing more, nothing less—just getting on base.

Beane took his limited payroll budget and sunk it all into guys who got on base. They didn't look like baseball stars, but his numbers told him that together they would win. That year the A's spent less than half of what the Yankees and Red Sox paid for players, but they made it to the play-offs. Logic and numbers trumped instinct and money in the 2002 Major League Baseball season.

It's about a balance: listening to and respecting both your base instincts and your rational mind. Sometimes my gut sends me messages, and I don't know exactly what to do with them. It takes time and brain work, but if your unconscious mind is sending you a strong message, it's worth your while to spend the brain power to turn it into a clear message.

Eriq La Salle, the actor from *ER* and *Coming to America,* had a house in the Hollywood Hills. It was his dream house, and a dream house built while he was one of the stars of the biggest show in prime time. He built the house so custom, so completely to his tastes, that it looked like a castle. Eriq was looking to sell the house for $9 million, but nobody was interested in the place. It was Eriq's dream, not theirs, so the price started to drop: $8 million, $7 million. I was not his agent, but I was watching the price drop and I was aware that an interesting prospect was shaping up.

The place has a great view, which means a lot in this market, but the style of the house was a very Spanish-Mediterranean look that's not super popular right now. Everyone walked into this $9 million, exquisitely appointed house and said, "It's great. It's just not for me." But I knew, somehow, this place was an opportunity. My gut was sending me a message, and I didn't quite know what it was yet.

I talked to Jeff, the head of my former company and one of my most important mentors. Jeff Hyland is an icon of Los Angeles real estate. He knows more about this market than anyone I've ever met. He has been working this town since 1975 and wrote the book *The Legendary Estates of Beverly Hills,* which details some of the biggest deals in the history of LA real estate. This guy is a walking Wikipedia of LA real estate stories, and most of them involve great stories about celebrities, so talking to him is always a good time. Since my gut was sending me a message I couldn't interpret, I figured Jeff would be the guy to push me in the right direction.

He told me in no uncertain terms that the house was the best deal on the market. I explained that the house had great high-quality fixtures and design, but nobody I took up there was falling in love with the place. If a person is going to spend $9 million on a place, they need to love it.

Jeff said, "With that view and that square footage, that place is a steal."

That's what I needed, some good old-fashioned Yoda-ing from Jeff. Things started to merge together in my mind. I started to see intellectually the factors my gut had sensed. I was looking at that house as a $9 million custom dream home, but it wasn't anymore. The house had fallen to $7 million. Maybe this wasn't a move-in or a remodel . . .

But $7 million is a lot to pay to just tear down a house and build a whole new one. And by now the house had been on the market for so long, people were starting to ignore it. No one was excited about this house anymore. My gut was telling me the price could go even lower. Jeff was right, that place was a great deal for the view and the square footage, but people didn't want the house itself. What if all we were selling was the view and the square footage? What if we leveled the place and built a new house? My brain figured out the course to monetize what my gut was telling me: this wasn't a $9 million custom castle; it was an over $6 million tear-down.

I talked to the seller's agent and felt around about Eriq's interest in moving the property, possibly at a lower price. The agent gave some indications it was possible. I called one of my deep-pocket developer buddies and told him about the place. That was a pretty high price tag for something I was pitching to him as a tear-down, so he said he was in but wouldn't go above $6 million. I was off and running. Offers and counteroffers were blasting back and forth. Finally, I was on the phone at the Whole Foods sandwich counter, yelling at Eriq's listing agent while I was yelling at the girl to put light mayo on my sandwich. I had them close, but they weren't dipping under $6 million.

Eriq's people were stuck at $6.05 million; my client wouldn't go over $6 million. I was trying to make a deal that kind of didn't make any sense to me: taking a beautiful, perfectly good house, buying it for a very healthy sum of money, then tearing it down to build a better house. Intellectually, I understood a lot of reasons I should maybe let the deal fall through and call it a day, but my gut was telling me this was the right choice. I said we had a deal at $6.05, then told my client I would put in the extra $50,000 from my commission.

Why? Because I believed in the deal. Because I knew that at the end of this deal was another, better deal with a new house that was taking full advantage of that lot and its view. My instinct and my vision had lined up, and it was worth my while to see that plan through.

The developer bought Eriq La Salle's place, tore it down, built a new house, and Matt and I are going to be listing it for sale at $25 million. We are going to make a full commission on that. That's what matters.

Following your gut isn't simply a matter of doing whatever you want. It's about maintaining a heightened state of awareness, then analyzing your instinctual reactions to be able to turn them into good decisions.

When other people saw Eriq La Salle's house, they were reacting to gut instincts too. They saw dark orange interiors and understood it wasn't somewhere they wanted to live. Real estate agents saw a place that didn't move for two years, and their guts told them that there must be something wrong with the place. What was the difference between their guts and mine?

Brains.

Your gut is constantly synthesizing a range of factors to create a base, fundamental opinion. It's your job to identify the factors that are contributing to that judgment and make sure you're giving the right importance to the right factors. That's the calculation part of calculated confidence: training yourself to trust your better instincts, and being able to pull apart and analyze a gut reaction when it isn't clear. Art historian Federico Zeri had learned enough about art to spot the tiny mistakes in that forged statue. Using his brain to feed and educate his instincts gave him better instincts than anybody else in the game.

I had a different instinct when it came to Eriq's house, but I also didn't know why. When I couldn't stop thinking about that house, and knew there was a deal there, I had to pull my instinct apart and figure out *why* I was reacting positively. The view, the lot, the price, the position of the seller, and the market were all vague, shifting factors I had to piece together. I had to use my own brain and Jeff Hyland's, but we figured out the appeal, and I was then able to structure a plan for execution.

You can't just trust your gut and expect that to solve every problem. Confidence alone isn't a guarantee of success either; very frequently it's a recipe for spectacular failure. Calculation is what's important to have the confidence that will pay off. Your gut can provide the big-picture direction, but your brain has to figure out the strategies that can make it possible.

You also need your head to keep you from falling for any gut instincts that are based on outdated ideas. If you're not constantly learning from the world around you, your gut's gonna be dumb. The scouts who were working for the A's before Billy Beane took over had dumb—or at least old-fashioned—guts. The real estate agents who ignored the possibilities of Eriq La Salle's house had dumb guts. If your brain is doing the work of keeping you informed about the stuff that matters in your life, your gut is going to steer you in the right direction. Once the decision is made, it's back to your brains to figure out the best strategies for execution.

Ultimately, if you let your gut be the godfather, directing and prioritizing your business, but you let your head be the consigliere, advising and strategizing execution, you won't be making decisions with blind confidence. You'll be making smart choices before you understand why they're smart.

12

It's Not Finished Until It's Finished

Coffee is for closers only.

—Blake (played by Alec Baldwin),
Glengarry Glen Ross
(screenplay by David Mamet)

This section of the book is about execution. Making calculated, confident decisions on the spur of the moment will only be successful if you pursue them until they are complete. Innovative ideas and exciting possibilities aren't going to pay your bills. It's your job to make sure that when you go after a deal, you close it. If you're going to fire, you have to do more than pull the trigger; you have to manage the consequences.

Good intentions don't get anything done. We all come out of New Year's with a plan to work out every morning. We plan an at-home business, maybe buy some of the stuff we'd need to start it, but most of the time, we never follow through. I can't tell you how many times I've bought groceries with the intention of making a big, beautiful dinner for my beautiful fiancée only to get home, get distracted, and find myself three weeks later throwing away some rotting filets mignons. That's half-assing it. That doesn't make anybody a millionaire (except the people selling the filets mignons).

If you like an idea enough to start it, like it enough to finish it. You have to pick your battles, but once you do, *fight*.

Fifteen years ago, Kellogg's had a good idea: People are busy. They miss breakfast a lot. Why not make a convenient, portable breakfast that gives them the whole grains and balanced nutrition of cereal with the convenience of a granola bar? In 1998, they created the Nutri-Grain bar, and it was a hit, particularly in the UK.

But brands have a life cycle, and once Kellogg's competitors in the UK started producing similar products and Nutri-Grain wasn't new or exciting anymore, the brand started to lose market share. By 2007, it looked like Nutri-Grain bars were dying in the UK.

Kellogg's could have looked at the facts that way, but instead they opted to see Nutri-Grain bars as an ongoing project that could continue to grow. They analyzed their market and found a few interesting facts:

- People were eating Nutri-Grain bars as a healthy snack all day long, not just as a breakfast replacement.

- Nutri-Grain bars were the only whole-grain snack bars on the market that were soft-baked.

- Nutri-Grain bars, with their fruity filling, felt a lot more indulgent that the granola and muesli bars they were competing against.

With these three facts, Kellogg's relaunched Nutri-Grain bars in the UK as an indulgent, anytime snack and really pushed the soft-baked branding. And they did one other thing to change people's perspectives: they stopped putting the bars on sale.

After ten years on the market, Nutri-Grain bars were a reliable staple for a lot of people. Something you grabbed when it was on sale but not a brand that felt special or exciting. After a decade on the shelves, Kellogg's wanted to make clear that Nutri-Grain was a brand you needed to get excited about.

It worked. Kellogg's turned a brand in decline into a success. They maintained a growth of Nutri-Grain bars that was three times the growth of the rest of the market for the following year. They followed through on their initial vision, and it paid off.[19]

In real estate, finishing the job is a big prospect. A house isn't a service that goes away. It's not a car that people get rid of in five years. It's a huge investment *and* the place where people live their lives. Continuing to be engaged with clients and provide them with ongoing service is a tall order, but one that can pay off in the long term.

---

had this one client, a Russian guy. He was leasing a place in Beverly Hills, wanted to get something permanent, looked around on some websites for a house in his price range, found one he liked, and called the listing agent. The listing agent was your old friend Josh Altman. I got a cold call from some guy I'd never heard of, telling me he was in the market for a place in Beverly Hills. I didn't know if he was legit or if he was some fifteen-year-old whose mom watched *Million Dollar Listing* and who could pull off a pretty sweet Russian accent.

So I met the guy to show him a property. He said he was an IT entrepreneur who'd just sold his company for $300 million. I called around and found out that the guy was legit, but I *also* found out he was looking at houses with every real estate agent in the 90210 zip code.

Matt and I found out about another house this client was interested in, so we called that agent to offer to join forces. We told the agent that he was looking all over town with a bunch of other agents, but if we worked together, we could guarantee this Russian guy would end up in either one of their houses or one of ours. The other agent was a guy very much on our level, and he was ready for the challenge. We agreed to split the commission.

We showed the client a dozen other houses. We did tons of legwork and felt *stupid* for agreeing to split the commission. Then he bought the one house the other agent had showed him, and Matt and I made half a commission instead of the no commission we would have made without the agreement.

But beyond that, we were building a relationship. We took him to Vegas to celebrate the sale, we had a good time, we became friends. Two weeks after everything closed, he went back to Russia to get his wife and start the process of moving to LA in earnest.

A week later, he called Matt. "Sell the house. We've decided to have a kid. We need a bigger house."

So now we had to turn around and sell the house he'd just bought. He'd paid $13.7 million. A week later, we got an offer for $14 million. I'm a pro, kids.

The dude said, "No." Matt and I were pretty pissed, considering a buyer who could make that house disappear for more than the man had paid for it was a pretty impressive find. The client said, "Yeah, but once I pay all the fees, I might lose some money."

Matt was *incensed*. We'd just seen this guy lose five hundred thousand dollars on one roll of the dice in Vegas. Why was he busting our balls about what would probably turn out to be a loss of a few thousand dollars?

"That was crazy. This is business."

That was all he had to say, and what's ridiculous is that's how most ridiculously rich people work. Billionaires nickel-and-dime me more than anyone else, and I have to respect it. That's how they became billionaires.

If Matt and I had simply let the other agent sell the client his house, pocketed our half of the commission, and moved along, we would have made some money. We didn't see that as the end of our job, though. We saw it as the beginning of a relationship. We'd built a friendship with the guy, and when he found out he was having a kid, we were the first people he thought of to sell his house *and* take him looking for bigger places.

In a game where we easily could have gotten no commission, we're going to get two and a half commissions.

———

Sometimes execution takes tenacity. Just because you can make a decision quickly doesn't mean you're going to be able to automatically get what you want. One of the ultimate examples of that for me was a lot Michael Strahan was developing in Bel Air.

First of all, Michael Strahan is a pretty amazing guy. Anyone who can go from fifteen years on the New York Giants to hosting a top-rated morning show is clearly a legend in the making.

Michael bought a place in Bel Air for $9 million where he was going to build his dream home. He had the money to fulfill his vision, and he was going to spare no expense. Unfortunately, people who don't work in development all the time don't always realize the labyrinth of red tape that you have to go through before you can get even the most basic construction done. While Michael was busy running the world from New York, building his dream home was moving down the list of priorities. As six months turned into a year, I could see they hadn't broken ground. I talked to his agent to see if Michael might want to just get rid of the property. He said, "No." Michael was still committed to building the house.

After Michael had spent over a year trying to get his plans approved, his agent relayed to me that there was a small window to put this deal together. This guy has multiple full-time jobs on both coasts; he doesn't have time to be haggling with architects and designers, who can never agree on anything.

Turns out it's a lot easier to just buy a house.

I made an offer on the place. Michael said no. I held back, waited a month, and made another offer. I had a developer who was interested, knew the game, and could guarantee a nice profit on the place. I made another offer. I was bargaining against myself, but Michael wasn't looking to sell. I was going to have to convince him. I offered $11.2 million. Michael was done, and five months after I started pestering him, he took the offer. My developer had the place and Michael made a $2 million–plus profit without having to dig a piece of dirt.

Great deals usually aren't easy. They usually take time, commitment, and planning to execute. You can't just trust that stuff is going to take care of itself. You have to be part of the deal the whole way through.

———————

Doing a job well enough doesn't impress anybody, including you. If you go through your life pursuing your decisions half-assed, the results are never going to be great, and you're going to lose your self-respect. Working hard is exhausting, yes, but it's the satisfied exhaustion of a job well done. If you treat your job as something to get through instead of something to excel at, you may have a bit more energy when you get home, but you won't have any sense of pride.

It's the steps past just getting the job done that create new business. It's refusing to accept the limitations of mediocrity and knowing you have the capacity to create excellence. You might have a business, a job, or a relationship that feels like it's done. It's your duty to look at it and figure out if there's something you want to salvage, and if so, create a plan to give it new life. You may have a task at work that seems limited and simple. If you do just that task and consider that to be enough and your job to be done, everyone you work with is going to think you're limited and simple.

Figure out how you can actualize all the potential of any deal. Execution is more than a series of tasks to get something you want. It's falling in love with a deal and the possibilities that surround it.

You remember when Tom Sawyer had to whitewash a fence? He talked loudly about how much fun it was to whitewash the fence, until some kids asked if they could help. He then convinced the kids to pay him money so they could have the chance to do his chore. That is, of course, genius-level salesmanship, but it's also getting the job done. Tom didn't just skip town or come up with a good excuse why he couldn't paint the fence. He looked at the job he had and found possibilities within it.

You don't have to swindle other people into doing your job for you. You need to swindle yourself and everyone around you into knowing that it is important to complete all aspects of a job. You have to fall in love with the details as much as you fell in love with the initial idea. It's a lot like Michael Strahan's house: You can't just come up with the plans for a really great house. You have to be fully committed to making your architect, planning commissioners, and contractors fall as much in love with the process as you are, and never stop until that dream house is built.

It's not finished until it's finished, and only you can decide when it's finished.

13

Always Kick the Football the Same

There are no menial jobs, only menial attitudes.

—William J. Brennan

As a high school and college football kicker, my whole job was one action. The rest of the team were these three-hundred-pound guys sweating and bleeding into the mud for every second of every game, and I was the guy in the clean little uniform, waiting to go out for thirty seconds to score a couple of points, then scamper back to the bench. I felt embarrassed for how limited my contribution to the team was.

As that guy who trotted onto the field once or twice per game—in some cases putting the whole outcome of the game on my shoulders (or toes)—it meant there was a lot of pressure on me to not screw it up. In these high-pressure situations, keeping my mind clear was almost impossible.

One summer, when I was in high school, my brother and I went to a kicking camp in Texas run by Ben Agajanian, the Dallas Cowboys' kicking coach. They call Ben "The Toeless Wonder" because he lost four toes in a workplace accident in college but still managed to play professional football for twenty years and win two NFL championships. (This was before they had Super Bowls.)

While we were at the camp, Ben said something that changed the way I looked at kicking, and deal making, for the rest of my life: "Always kick the football the same."

It sounds like non-advice. It sounds stupid. It sounds obvious. It is, however, one of the best pieces of advice I've ever gotten (second only to my father's sage words "Don't get her pregnant").

What Coach Agajanian said was simple but so profound. If I let my brain get caught up in the possible consequences of my actions, I was not focused and I would be susceptible to intimidation. If I focused on the task at hand, on letting my kick be just as good or just as bad as all the other kicks I'd taken in practice, I would be freeing myself up. I was a good kicker. I'd practiced, trained, and studied everything I could to get good. If I just did my job like I knew how to do it, I'd be fine, but if I let myself become too aware of the consequences, I would lose focus.

When I was thirteen and still playing soccer, we were in a really tight game, down 1–2. As the final seconds ticked down, a guy tripped me. The ref called a foul, told everyone to leave the field, and gave me one final penalty kick. That was it. If I missed, we lost. If I made it, we tied. To this day I can remember running up toward that ball, making impact, it flying through the air, rolling off the goalie's fingers, and hitting the net. It's like a movie moment. Sure, in a movie we would have won the game, and the guy kicking the ball would have been a little taller, but I know what it's like to be in a high-pressure moment like that and have everything go right.

Which makes every other high-pressure situation even more scary.

After that penalty kick, every time I went to kick for a penalty in soccer or an extra point or a field goal, I knew what success would feel like, and I was filled with the crushing knowledge that this time it could go wrong.

When you're doing a job, don't focus on the variables outside of your control. Focus on execution, do that job well, and trust that this task is part of a larger strategy you've already worked out. Second-guessing your strategy when it's too late doesn't help anyone.

Do the job in front of you well.

A couple of years ago, a young woman called me up and said she wanted me to find her a lease. Now, real estate agents *hate* lease clients. A real estate agent doesn't make that much money off a lease. It's just as much work as finding someone a house, with almost no payoff. And it wasn't easy; this client could not be pleased. I took her around to condo after condo for the better part of four months. You might be wondering why I spent that much time working a job that, in the end, wasn't going to pay me off. Well, the fact that she was a cute blonde in her early thirties didn't hurt, but the main reason was just that when I do a job, I do it right. I approach all jobs with the same level of discipline and tenacity. I kick the ball the same way.

You guys have seen in earlier chapters of this book that my dedication to good, exhaustive service frequently results in me getting return business. This was not a situation where that was even remotely imaginable. This was a young woman at the beginning of her career who would probably never be buying a high-end home in West LA. The most business I could hope to get out of her was a year later, when she needed someone to drive her around for four more months, hunting after another rental.

Or so I thought . . .

I found the woman the lease she was looking for, set her up, and got her into the place. She told her parents how great I had been. Turns out her dad was a top executive with a major corporation, and after talking on the phone with his baby girl, he went to dinner with his CEO. A CEO who happened to need someone to sell his penthouse on Ocean Avenue in Santa Monica. And guess who that CEO listed his gorgeous penthouse with? This guy.

For those of you who don't live in LA, Ocean Avenue is the road that runs just above the Pacific Coast Highway, the most beautiful stretch of coastline in the world. This condo was literally hanging on a cliff over the beach. Because the complex is on a cliff, the penthouse isn't on the top floor; it's on the bottom, so you're perched just above the ocean. The listing was *huge,* and it was mine.

So I listed the place and had an open house. When you're holding an open house at a property that high end, you're looking to sell it, yeah, but you're also looking to make contact and build relationships with the people who are coming through. Sure, some people are just there to gawk at where the rich people live, but most of the people are rich and looking for a house. It's my happy hunting ground. At this particular open house was a celebrity dermatologist who's made millions off his skin-care line. Luckily, I'm blessed with naturally flawless skin, but I knew *exactly* who he was. We started talking, and he let me know he liked this condo, but it was a little small. He told me he needed a place just as high end, with a view that was just as beautiful, but twice the size.

"I've got the perfect place to show you!" I lied. Of course I lied. Always have a house to show.

Matt and I sold the Ocean Avenue condo for $3.8 million, but now I had the much bigger task of finding a place to show "Dr. Stars." It was intimidating. This guy was talking about spending $7 to $8 million on a condo. That's a big commission. I could have gotten worried I was out of my depth and started panicking. I didn't. I kicked the football the same.

I started searching around, trying to find anything that might be in the right range for Dr. Stars. I found out that a wealthy family in the fashion business was looking to downsize from their condo. It was an 8,000-square-foot condo. For those of you who aren't great with numbers, what that means is *huge*. If it were in Manhattan, it'd be one of the ten biggest condos available. It was gorgeous and it had a perfect 360-degree Santa Monica view of the ocean. It was a lot of apartment.

But there's more. The place also had an 8,000-square-foot deck right on top of it. This was 16,000 square feet of apartment on top of a Santa Monica high-rise that let you look down on some of the most beautiful geography God ever made. The fashion family had bought the place for $8 million. I would get my client the best possible price, but I knew this was going to be one huge sale.

I could have been nervous, I could have been overwhelmed, but I knew that everything in this sale was just a bigger version of everything I'd done before. I'd dealt with the superrich, with celebrities, and with high-cost properties. I had all the skills I needed; I just had to kick that ball.

Dr. Stars bought it for $11.25 million. What started out as a four-month chase to find a minor client the right $1,700-a-month lease had turned into the biggest sale for a condo in the history of Santa Monica. We also sold her parents a house for $3.25 million, we sold the CEO a new condo, and through the other people we've met through them, I've sold $24 million in real estate. If I'd treated that first woman like a throw-away client, I would have lost out on a major commission, and I also wouldn't have found and developed these other relationships that have paid me handsomely. It was the cute blonde looking for the endless lease who ironically became the one who laid the golden egg.

When you half-ass a job, you're hurting yourself. You're hurting your reputation. Your reputation exists outside of you, in the world, informing people about the job you do. You can have the best plans and intentions for any deal or job, but if your reputation isn't out there convincing people, you may never get the chance to prove your abilities.

And your reputation doesn't just affect the way others see you; it also affects the way you understand yourself. Going at every job with a consistency of quality makes you sure that you're capable of doing it right every time. Half-assing your job is a way of insulating yourself from failure. You imagine that you're only doing inferior quality work because the situation doesn't demand it, that if something worthy of your skills really came up, you could kill it. If you take that approach, you're never going to be ready for the big kicks. The only way to take on a big task is if you've already proven to yourself a thousand times that you can do the job. Consistency reminds *you* how good you are.

Your life is going to be full of big opportunities and small ones, good times and rough ones. Those things change in ways you can't fully control. The one thing you can control is *you*. You can believe that you don't need to be ready all the time, that when a big chance comes along, you'll choose to kill it, but frequently the chances come in ways you won't recognize. I didn't know that woman was going to lead to huge paydays, and if I hadn't given her top-quality service, I never would have known it. Those doors would have remained closed and I would have thought I was just some guy who never got the chance to prove myself.

You prove yourself every day. The tiny little choices that define your life add up to your character. If you build your character into something you can be proud of, you'll open up opportunities other people wouldn't have seen. You'll make smart choices before you realize their full impact. If you build a strong character, there won't be any big presentations or make-or-break sales meetings you have to sweat over, because you'll have spent your career treating every sales meeting and presentation like they matter. Because they do matter.

Calculated confidence is a skill built through consistency. It's having enough practice under your belt to be able to make big, decisive calls in high-pressure situations.

You have to kick every football like it matters, so that when you're in a situation when everyone around you is freaking out, yelling, cheering, or otherwise giving you stimulus that could make anyone anxious, you know how to just do your job.

No deal is going to break me. No failure is going to ruin my life, make my fiancée not love me, or make my parents not be proud of me. My worth isn't this one deal or this one kick. My value is my character, my skill, and my fight. What matters isn't the situation around the ball—the tied football game, the $11.25 million condo sale, or whatever. The reason you always kick the ball the same is because the ball doesn't matter. Who's kicking the ball matters.

14

Remember the Big Picture

Happiness is not a matter of
intensity but of balance and order
and rhythm and harmony.

—Thomas Merton

Okay, that quote is maybe taking things a little far. We know I'm a guy who likes intensity. I enjoy succeeding and tend to structure my whole life in ways that will facilitate me taking my career to the next level.

Remembering the big picture in a business environment is key to breaking away from ingrained policies that do nothing to make us more productive.

Taking your career to the next level depends on you being able to see the bigger picture, just as Sidney Harman did. Back

in the late '60s, Harman had two jobs: he was the CEO of Harman Kardon, a sound system manufacturer, and the president
of an experimental college on Long Island, Friends World
College. The college was run according to Quaker philosophy. Students were supposed to educate themselves; it was the
professors' job to facilitate that process. Education didn't flow
from the top down; it was a collaborative effort the students
were fundamentally in charge of.

So Harman was bouncing back and forth between these two
jobs until he got a call in 1968 telling him that there was a crisis
at one of Harman Kardon's plants in Tennessee. He went down
to investigate and found out that the entire problem was the re-
sult of a broken buzzer. See, the factory ran twenty-four hours
a day, and the night shift in the polish-and-buff department got
a coffee break at ten P.M. When the buzzer—which notified the
men of their break—broke, management postponed the break
until a time when another buzzer sounded.

Eventually, one employee got annoyed with the whole process. He said that he could figure out when it was ten P.M. just
fine and started taking his coffee break then. The other men
in the department followed suit. The management was pissed
and ready to start punishing the men for their insubordination.

Sidney Harman came down and took in the whole situation.
It could have been solved, very simply, by fixing the buzzer,
but Harman saw that this tiny, avoidable crisis was reflective of
something very different. See, those twelve guys in the polish-
and-buff department were mostly black. It was the South in
1968, and racial dynamics in the country were shifting rapidly.
Black Americans who had suffered indignities for centuries
were sticking up for themselves.

And the factory's management was being stupid. They were structuring a day around their technology instead of using technology to facilitate their workers. In Harman's words, "The technology is there to serve the men, not the reverse."

So Harman started restructuring his factory to look a lot more like that Quaker college campus he was in charge of. He offered classes and piano lessons to the workers; he started letting the workers publish a newsletter, where they were free to criticize and make fun of the management; and he let the factory workers take the lead in running their workplace.[20]

Harman didn't come to see a problem and solve it; he came to a factory in crisis, he looked at the entire business as a living society, and he worked to make it better for everyone involved. He saw the big picture.

When it comes to real estate, I think I'm pretty good at keeping the big picture in mind. No one deal is going to make or break me. It's about maintaining a career. My professional reputation and character are worth way more than a single deal, and it pays off to conduct all my business in a way I can be proud of.

My friend Ilan is a pretty regular fixture on *Million Dollar Listing*. We met at a party in Hollywood. Somebody said, "This dude is building a house," and I introduced myself, because if you're involved in real estate in any way, you need to know me. He had a decent chunk of money from a background in marketing and merchandising, and his parents had clued him in to an old lady in the Hollywood Hills who was getting rid of her house.

He'd gotten a place for $600,000 that was easily worth $1.2 million. The dude had natural talent, it seemed. And despite being my age and dressing very normally, I soon discovered that Ilan had almost endless financial resources. This was a guy I could work with.

He was building an East Coast traditional house, and I started stopping by once every few weeks to check in, just to let him know the kind of service I'd be providing. We listed the house, put it on the market, had one showing, got an offer, got them up to full price, and closed sixty days later. We never had another showing; that was it. We found the one buyer who was interested in the house. One and done. Ilan had bought a tear-down, so his total investment was somewhere around $2 million. We sold it for $4.5 million. That's how you do business.

So now Ilan and I work together all the time. I've sold him eleven houses now, and he's a good friend and a top client. I could build my career around a couple of top clients like Ilan, and all the time other agents are trying to show him stuff. He'll call me up and tell me someone's offered to show him a pocket listing. That's a listing that's so upscale and boutique, it's not going formally on the market. It's essentially invite-only real estate.

I could be difficult about something like this. I could be territorial and possessive. That might keep Ilan from pursuing that one listing, but in the long run, he'd start wondering why I was so nervous about him working with other real estate agents. I have to look at the big picture. Ilan's business means a lot to me, so I need to give him the respect to let him pursue other opportunities while trusting my level of care and service will keep him coming back.

God, with all this talk of servicing and respecting someone and loving them enough to let them go, you'd think I'd be better at relationships.

That's the thing. In my personal life, I'm not that great at stepping back and weighing the importance of various factors. I like succeeding in business *so* much that I can forget how much succeeding in my personal life satisfies me.

The worst part is that my fiancée, Heather, is just as professionally focused as I am. We're two very career-oriented people in the same business working for the same company. It means that when we work together, we are an awesome and devastating force, and it means getting us to turn off our phones and pay attention to each other can be really, really hard. But we have to, because life is worth living.

When you're growing up, you look at adults with their cars and houses and money, and you want that. You want the freedom and options that come with money, so you work for it, you fight for it. Eventually, with some of us, the fight takes over. You start to love the fight the way you used to, let's say, love a new car. That's beautiful. It makes you a business machine who's constantly working to make this country's economy bigger and better.

But you can't be a machine all day every day. You're a person, you need to relax, you need to feel love, and you need to show love to the people around you. If you try to live like a machine, eventually you'll break down. Live like a human being and you can grow, thrive, and be happy.

That's what I tell myself while I'm pouring enough coffee down my throat to keep going for a twelfth house showing on a Tuesday.

I lose touch with the big picture when I stress out. Time is my biggest struggle during the day, and when I get caught up in anything that I feel is unnecessarily wasting my time, I start to get on edge. Tiny, annoying, time-consuming tasks can get in my way and frustrate me no end. Don't get me wrong. These tasks are necessary, maybe even important; I just don't want to have to deal with them personally, because they're usually things somebody just needs to show up for. I hate doing busy work when I could be out there excelling.

The trouble is, messing around with those tasks, like being around for house inspections or managing the paperwork, gets in my head. I'm so aware of the time I feel like I'm "wasting" that when I actually can go get into my car and move on with the rest of my day, I'm not working as clearly or as efficiently as I should be.

The reason is cortisol. It's a hormone that is released when you're under stress, when you don't get enough sleep, and when you drink coffee. It is, of course, terrible for you. It makes you gain weight in your belly, weakens your immune system, and even weakens your bones. I know I'm a stress junkie and the worst person to say this, but keeping yourself in a high-stress state all the time screws with your ability to make smart decisions.

A Dutch neuroscientist, Dr. Ruud van den Bos, found that people with heightened cortisol levels tend to make high-risk decisions and seek short-term gains.[21] So when I'm in these time-sucking activities and I get a phone call from someone asking me to do a speaking engagement, I sometimes agree to it without thinking it out fully, because I'm just trying to get them off the phone. On a couple of occasions, this has led to real scheduling difficulties that could have been avoided if I'd made the decision with a cool, logical head.

Keeping yourself stressed out is like a recipe for making bad decisions. If you want to be able to trust your confident decision-making abilities, you have to keep your job and life in perspective and take care of yourself.

When I'm at work, I'm an attack dog. I get every penny that I can for my clients, and I take pride in it. However, when I go to buy a car for myself, I'm the world's worst negotiator. Heather always makes fun of me about it. The car guy tells me the price of a car, I say "Sure," and then, on the ride home, Heather's so confused and frustrated that I didn't negotiate.

"He mentioned that he was getting a divorce. You could have just walked away, gotten him scared and gotten the price down by ten grand!"

That's the thing about having a real true partner in life. She knows the game as well as I do. I just don't play it for myself. Maybe I should give enough love and energy to my private life so I can bring the fight to negotiations over a car for myself. The way I see it, life is short. I fight tooth and nail for my clients every day. When it comes to me getting an awesome car, I'm willing to just pay the extra money and drive home in peace.

———

The ultimate big picture moment of my life happened this year. Last year, I got engaged to Heather. She's the love of my life, my partner professionally and personally, and I wanted her to know that I want to share the rest of my life with her.

What I forgot was that I was also on a reality show. *Million Dollar Listing* is great. It's built my career and my ego to heights I never could have dreamed of. Heather's my partner in that too. She's also on the show, and she knows what it's like to try to balance a very real business with a reality show that's always trying to put some extra Hollywood polish on our lives.

So the minute I got engaged to Heather, things started moving toward a wedding . . . fast. We weren't just going to have *a* wedding; we were going to have *the* wedding. A Hollywood reality show wedding. Maybe we weren't Kim and Kanye, but we could at least be Tamra and Eddie from *Real Housewives of Orange County*.

Heather's from Las Vegas. This means she grew up with a very jaded view of the wedding industry. She's allergic to the idea of a big wedding. Most guys' dream, right? But I had committed to us serving up a grand, impressive spectacle for the show, and I only gave myself three months to do it.

I was headed toward completing my task with the aggression and tenacity I bring to my work life. I was going to *kill* this wedding so Bravo would like it, so people at home would like it, so everyone would know how much I love Heather Bilyeu.

The one person I wasn't thinking about was Heather.

That's ridiculous, I know. It's not how relationships work, I know. But I'm being honest. While we were both working our asses off to manage a growing company, I'd decided we also had to take on the job of planning and organizing a wedding that was primarily going to exist to provide added production value to a TV show.

Most women *love* weddings, but to Heather, they're a way of making promises that should be proven by day-to-day behavior. When it comes to love, she wants substance over symbols. She was going through with the wedding because it's what I wanted, but she was getting frustrated. Every day she had to take two hours out of her work schedule to meet with a wedding planner, she frayed just a little bit more. Finally, she broke. We both broke.

We didn't have it in us to throw together a big showy wedding in three months. Screw that. We knew we could *produce* a wedding in three months, but that'd be work, us doing a job. We could do that. What we couldn't create in three months was *our* wedding: a wedding for us, one that was a representation and celebration of our relationship. I know you think I'm just the little cocky man on your TV screen, but there's a full-size, real-life me that has a life and a fiancée, and sometimes that has to come first.

So we cancelled our wedding. We'd already shot a bunch of footage of us planning the thing; we couldn't pretend like it never happened. We had to cancel our wedding *on national television* with all the implications about our relationship that go along with that. In front of our family, strangers, and the girls who'd talked shit about Heather in junior high. It sucked.

But life is more than a TV show. It's more than a real estate deal, and it's more than a real estate business. There's a whole big picture to worry about, and the biggest thing in my picture is my relationship with Heather. It may have looked sketchy to you guys watching at home, but I can't worry about that.

If I'm gonna be happy, healthy, and capable of making good decisions, I need to keep some balance in my life. The balance in my life is named Heather Bilyeu, and one day soon she'll be Heather Bilyeu-Altman. People at home may not get to watch it, but I don't care. Some things are just for us.

Part Three

Aim

We all want lives that are perfect. Every fender bender, dropped egg, or missed bus can send us into a spiral about what might have been if we'd only been a little bit better or more prepared. We all wish we could change the past, to fix this mistake or that one, but the simple truth is that we can't, and we shouldn't. Those mistakes taught us lessons.

Every kid has to get burned once. He or she will never really understand the dangers of fire until it happens, and after it does, that kid will never really forget the potential pain. Succeeding in life isn't about being a perfect person who avoids all bad decisions; it's about getting burned once, then being smart enough to avoid getting burned in the future. We all have to learn these lessons for ourselves. You have to pay for the extended warranty, you have to date the super-attractive narcissist, you have to buy tickets to Costa Rica without checking when "the rainy season" is. That's life.

You can't hate yourself for being human. That's a waste of time and energy. It's easy to convince yourself that the people around you don't make mistakes, and that their lives are unfettered drives toward success and happiness. We all know that isn't true. We're all fallible creatures just working to make our way through life and get a little smarter in the process.

The answer to mistakes isn't to get mad at yourself; it's to learn. You have to look at the mistake and analyze what happened. You can't let a bruised ego get in the way of honestly looking at the mistake and evaluating what contributed to it. Figure out how you could have done better, and if that was even possible. If it was, move forward a little smarter and more prepared for the world.

Trying too hard to protect yourself from unforeseen circumstances is a great way to keep yourself from ever really trying at anything. Caution is valuable when it's specific and concrete. When it's vague, it stops being caution and becomes fear, which stops you from being able to fire at a moment's notice. Aiming is about collecting important experiences that hone your gut instincts and allow you to make subtler, more accurate calculations to support your confidence.

The simple truth is, knowing about a problem can inform your decisions, but living through a mistake will guide your instincts. If you know intellectually that a stove is hot, you'll avoid it as long as you're thinking about it, but once you've actually burned yourself, your conscious and unconscious minds work together to keep you from doing it again. I'm not saying you should try to encounter failure. I'm just saying you will, and when you do, work very hard to find the lessons in the failure.

I've had a career with a lot of amazing highs but also some really crushing lows. As someone who espouses the importance of confidence in business and life, I find it embarrassing to say it was astoundingly hard to find my confidence in those low moments. You too can wear all the fancy suits you like and decide to make your own luck, but in some moments, it can feel like you've got nothing left to move forward with.

Those are the moments when you have to fight, to put one foot in front of the other and get back on the path toward your goal, now with the wisdom and insight gained from your mistake. You have to aim yourself a little more precisely at your goal and get moving again.

If you keep moving forward and refining your aim, nothing can stop you. I'm not saying you'll definitely be a millionaire, and I'm not saying you won't run into more setbacks, but as long as you keep pushing yourself and being smart about where you're going, your life will keep getting better.

15

Risk Smart,
Not Hard

Get wisdom—how much
better it is than gold!

—Proverbs 16:16

This is the part of the book where I talk about my mistakes. That's nobody's idea of a good time. Reliving the various screwups you've committed in life is a great way to end the day hating yourself. You just wish that back then you would've known more, been better, somehow been able to dodge the stupid mistake that screwed up your life.

That's why you have to look at your mistakes. To aim. To be prepared the next time the same kind of opportunity for a screwup comes your way, and be able to dodge it. I'm not a great real estate agent because I never made mistakes. I'm a great real estate agent because I made huge mistakes, *huge* mistakes, and then learned from them. I vowed never to make the same kind of mistake again. You can't be shell-shocked or paranoid. You can't spend your life being damaged by one screwup you went through at the beginning of your career. You have to grow up, be a businessperson, and look at the mistake clinically.

Look at your mistakes until they stop hurting; only then will you be able to start learning the lessons they have to teach you.

One of the biggest, stupidest risks of all time was taken by one of the biggest, most powerful brands in the world. Coca-Cola—the brand so powerful it's what Andy Warhol used when he commented on branding in American culture—decided it needed to change its formula. If you're over thirty, you remember this; if you're under thirty, it'll barely make sense.

In 1985, Coca-Cola was the world's leader in carbonated beverages. It was on top, but it'd lost some market share to Pepsi, which tasted a little bit sweeter. Pepsi was leaning heavily on generational marketing, saying it was "The Choice of a New Generation" and plugging blind taste tests that said people preferred the taste of Pepsi.

So Coca-Cola, with a winning product that wasn't going anywhere, decided it needed to change its formula. The company launched "new Coke," a sweeter product in a newly designed can. The familiar script "Coca-Cola" was replaced with a thick block: "Coke." People went apeshit.

You're probably wondering how a behemoth of a company like Coca-Cola managed to make a mistake this big. Didn't the company do research? Of course it researched the hell out of new Coke, and found it consistently beat both Pepsi and classic Coca-Cola in taste tests. But when the company's researchers asked consumers if they would buy the drink if it *were* classic Coca-Cola, the focus groups reacted like the researchers were speaking blasphemy. The research response to new Coke was essentially "You're not my real dad!"

Coca-Cola simply could not understand the iconic power of its brand. The company saw simple numbers that showed the new drink formula was more likable. What the researchers heard in focus groups was confusing, so they ignored it.

Coca-Cola was ready and willing to throw away a hundred years of branding, customer loyalty, and developed tastes to try to compete with a company without its prominence. If its brand had been less strong, it might have simply innovated itself out of existence. Instead, the loyal consumers of Coca-Cola took to the streets to demand the return of the product they knew and loved. Coca-Cola's place in the American mythos was gal-vanized. Pepsi might insist it was the choice of a new generation, but Coca-Cola—now labeled "Coca-Cola classic"—was the taste of America's greatest century. Two months after the launch of new Coke, Coca-Cola classic was returned to the shelves.

Coca-Cola took a *huge* risk with their rebranding attempt. It's one of the rare situations where a major corporation risked everything on an idea. It did not help that the idea was terrible. The risk was such a mess that many people now insist it must have been a conspiracy to distract drinkers from the switch from sugar to high-fructose corn syrup or to rally enthusiasm for the original Coca-Cola formula.

What I'm saying is don't do that. Don't risk everything you have on an opportunity unless you are absolutely sure it's the best and only choice. I'm not saying you should fear failure; I'm saying you should keep your risks limited and smart enough that you don't have to fear failure. Going to Las Vegas and putting your entire life's savings on red 23 is a bold choice, yes, but thirty-seven out of thirty-eight times, it's going to be the stupidest move you could possibly make.

Believe me, I know what I'm talking about. Even arrogant old Josh Altman knows what it's like to let hubris get the better of him. Back when I was running my own mortgage refinance company, I was making a lot of money, and flipping houses was making me even more money. Matt and I flipped the condo, and we flipped a few houses in marginal neighborhoods. We'd dealt with stuff in the $900,000 to $1.1 million range. In my head, we knew exactly what we were doing, and between my job as a mortgage broker and Matt working at the CAA (Creative Artists Agency), we had the resources to take on a bigger, fancier house and have even bigger returns. I wanted to play with the big boys!

I was, of course, spending every spare moment checking the MLS and going to see houses. I came across one that captured my imagination. Everything we'd flipped before had been a condo or a nice, responsible family home down in the flats of LA. This one was a glorious Spanish mansion in Laurel Canyon. It had everything: 4,000 square feet, four bedrooms, three and a half baths, two master suites. We're talking $50,000 hand-carved wood ceilings, Gothic windows, a huge tile balcony, and (it came with the furniture) a gigantic, sixteen-person wooden dining table. It even had a name: El Castillo. I needed this place. My imagination was consumed with what our lives would be like if we lived there, and just how much money we could make on flipping the place.

Now, you're probably saying "Hey, Altman, what exactly did two guys in their twenties need with a four-bedroom Spanish castle in Laurel Canyon?" You're getting ahead of the story.

We made an offer and bought it in 2007 for $2.175 million. It was a huge mortgage; our monthly payment would be $11,000. My brother Matt wasn't certain we could afford it, but I, the business genius whose book you bought, said, "Don't worry. I make $50,000 a month. I can pay that off in four days of work." I told him I'd pay more than my half of the mortgage. What could go wrong?

We closed in June of 2007. A little something called the subprime mortgage crisis started to go down six months later.

The bubble burst, the bubble we had been riding with all our house flips. Also, the bubble that had allowed me to sell mortgage refinances to hundreds of people whose house values had been artificially inflated by the market. Suddenly, everyone's house was worth half of what it had been worth six months before.

I was making a great income when we bought the house, yes, but my entire income was based on commissions for refinances. By 2008, nobody was able to get a mortgage approved. My business withered. I had to let go of my employees. I kept pounding the phones, but as time went on, it became clear there was no point. The mortgage refinance business was, for the immediate future, dead.

Winter is a hard time. It gets dark early. It gets cold. Well, in LA it doesn't get cold so much as it gets charmingly mild. However beautiful LA is year-round, the winter of 2007–2008 was one of the hardest times in my life. Then it started to pour.

Matt and I had done a fair amount of remodeling on the places we had flipped but had never dealt with extras that come with a high-end, multimillion-dollar home. We'd lived in the Laurel Canyon house for six months and never had any problem, but after hosting several parties at our home, showing off our cool elevator, and blasting the air-conditioning 24/7, the shortcomings of this house became shockingly clear. Having an elevator seems really cool, until it breaks down and Lago, the elevator repairman, shows up not just late but days late to repair it—then it becomes a bit of a nuisance and gouges the bank account significantly.

We could not afford this house. With barely any income, the mortgage was chewing up my savings and spitting it out. The cars I'd bought when things were going well just sat there, reminding me of what an idiot I'd been. Back before the mortgage meltdown, Matt and I had awesome dinner parties on that giant medieval table. All our friends had been shocked that we had a house like this. "How do you guys live here?" had filled me with pride when they'd said it in the summer of 2007, but by 2008, that house was my biggest shame. For the first time in my life, I felt like I wasn't in control of what was happening to me.

The summer of 2008, we put the house on the market. I thought our supercool house was going to move immediately. Nothing happened. The banks had completely tightened up; no one could get a mortgage anymore. Any developer who might have enough money to get the place was savvy enough to have the proper inspections done and realize the place was a potential money pit.

Matt and I were screwed. Oh, except for that thing where I'd said I'd take care of the mortgage. I was screwed.

We were desperate to move the place, which turned us into the worst clients any real estate agent could imagine. Any good real estate agent will tell owners to get out of the house and let potential buyers see it empty. You let the buyers imagine *their* life in the house, not see the reality of yours. Any time Matt and I saw someone interested in the place, we'd invite them over for dinner to try to sell them on the house. Of course it never worked. And of course our agent was getting frustrated with us. We'd constantly call after every showing and open house, stalking our agent, asking, "What was the feedback?" The common theme was "No one wants to live in a dark castle." This house was so specific. LA is full of beautiful Santa Barbara Spanish homes, contemporary and traditional, not castles. We were screwed.

We had to do something drastic, so we finally decided to do something smart. We took it off the market, rolled up our sleeves, and started renovating to deal with the broken elevator and air-conditioning and improve the home aesthetically. Well, let's be honest: Matt and I paid other people to roll up their sleeves, but it cost us a decent chunk of money. The way I saw it, if that house was going to devour all of my savings, at the end at least I would have a house that wasn't dark and depressing and I could spend my jobless days riding my elevator.

We did have one asset to leverage: that house. So during the months when we were fixing it up, I started renting it out. A friend had told me that in LA you could make decent money by renting your place out as a location for movies or parties. Or if things got really bad, porn. We never got to the porn point, but we came close. If nothing else, we pimped that house out hard enough for it to pay at least some of our bills.

I hadn't entirely learned my lesson about risking smart, though. In February of 2009, I decided I was going to make some money off Valentine's Day by doing a pop-up rose shop in Beverly Hills. I hooked up with a florist, who assured me I could quadruple my money, so I bought twenty-five thousand dollars' worth of roses the day before Valentine's Day, set up shop, and watched as absolutely no one bought our flowers.

Then I learned that when you're selling flowers, you can't keep your inventory. By the end of the day on February 14, I had a bunch of flowers on my hands that were just going to die. Matt and I called all our friends to come snag some for their ladies, and I, finally, started to realize that big bold risks might not be all it takes to succeed in business.

After a year of hard work on the house, we had lightened, brightened, and de-castlefied it, gotten air-conditioning that worked, and fixed the elevator. That's a harsh moment, when you realize the very impressive stupidity required for a dude in his twenties to buy a house with its own elevator, then multiply that by buying a house with an elevator that doesn't work. It was humbling, but by 2010, the market was starting to recover and the house was in much better shape.

In real estate, it only takes one buyer, and thankfully we finally found him. He made an offer. It was nearly $200,000 less than what we'd paid for the house, and it didn't in any way cover the money we'd spent on improving it, but this was our chance to get out and we took it.

That house could have bankrupted me. It was a stupid, stupid risk, but in the process of facing my mistake, I learned about houses. There is now no possible way I would ever consider buying a house that is so custom and specific. That Spanish castle clued me in to all the unseen dangers that can exist in a house, especially when buying such a specific home, but that a savvy buyer can find.

I made a stupid, stupid mistake and lost hundreds of thousands of dollars in the process. I'm not proud of it, but I'm proud of what I learned from it. Yeah, I fired too soon, at too big of a target, but that mistake just gave me the knowledge I needed to aim to be better.

Plus, that was a *really* cool table.

16

Embrace Rejection

> We all learn lessons in life. . . . I have always
> learned more from rejection and failure
> than from acceptance and success.
>
> **—Henry Rollins**

I love America, but I worry about it. Our great-grandparents
rolled over to Europe, slogged through the mud, and beat the
Kaiser; then our grandparents went back, stormed Normandy,
and took down Hitler. My parents' generation pushed forward
the biggest expansion of the U.S. economy in history and made
us the undisputed superpower of the world. They took down
segregation, they fought for women's rights, and they made this
a country we could be prouder of. They fought.

We don't like kids fighting anymore. We have Little League games where nobody wins so no one feels bad. We show them movies where fights never have any blood or consequences. There's lots of sharing, lots of caring, and no negative consequences.

We're starting to get the first crop of this Millennial generation in the workplace. After lives where they were constantly told how special and important they are, they're finally facing a world that doesn't give two shits about them. They're very creative and technically savvy, but they're going to have to learn some big lessons about dealing with rejection to succeed in business. This isn't a game where everyone wins.

The other day I went to meet with a seller who was looking for an agent. He'd been meeting with a couple of different guys, so it was my job to tap dance and impress him. I was in one of my classic time-stress moods, and I barreled in, there to make my skills known as quickly and efficiently as possible. The guy asked me how much his house was worth.

I said, "$4.9."

He nodded and I left.

Later that day, he called to tell me I hadn't gotten the listing. He said, "I was looking to hear a number around $5.4."

At first, I was pissed. That house was worth $4.9 million. Those other agents were blowing smoke up that guy's ass. I was the good agent. I was the honest agent. How *dare* he reject me?

Then I remembered: *it's my job to blow smoke up that guy's ass.*

When a patient goes to see a surgeon, the surgeon doesn't explain all the harsh, terrible things she's going to have to do during the operation. She tells the patient what the patient needs to know in terms that will make sense to him. As a cold-blooded real estate professional, I can tell you that $4.9 million was what that house was *actually* going to go for. But as an experienced real estate agent, I also need to remember to have some degree of bedside manner. Houses have sentimental value. They're filled with people's memories. No one wants to hear their house broken down to its most basic worth. The process of listing a house is more complex than that. You put a house on the market at a price the seller feels is appropriate, then once the market makes clear that it won't move at that price, you talk to him about lowering it.

Sometimes it might come off as annoying and tedious, but that's my job, to understand not just what a house is worth but also how invested a seller is in it.

Rejection is full of lessons.

There's a story of Thomas Edison explaining the long series of trial and error that went into inventing the first lightbulb, resulting in thousands of prototypes before getting it right. One of the listeners expressed surprise that he'd continued even though he'd failed all those times. Edison replied that he had not failed. He had succeeded in finding thousands of ways that didn't work.

You're not failing, you're learning. Every choice is an experiment, and every experiment gives you new information. Unless, of course, you're making the same mistake over and over and over again. That doesn't give you new information. It just means you're probably smoking a lot of pot.

Matthew Epstein got rejected a lot. He was a twenty-four-year-old with a couple of years of tech marketing jobs under his belt. He was looking to take the next step in his career, but for all the résumés he sent out, he got no replies. The Internet has made it way, way easier for employers to just ignore people harassing them about a job.

Matthew got fed up. He applied the way he was supposed to apply, but the companies just ignored him. Then he realized that he was a person applying for a job in tech marketing; his skill set was supposed to involve creating messages that are hard to ignore. He also realized that if the Internet makes it easy for employers to ignore him, it could also make it way easier for him to get their attention.

So he had the audacity to just say what he wanted. He built a website called GooglePleaseHire.Me. The site included a video of Matthew strutting around a mansion in a fake moustache and business suit and talking about his desire for a job at Google with a parade of ridiculous jokes. Under the video were two clear, simple buttons: one to look at Matthew's résumé, the other to get in contact. Matthew had created a forum that clearly and engagingly articulated his message, then provided a simple way to follow up. That's how marketing works.

A bunch of tech companies had ignored the résumé where Matthew had just said he was good at marketing, so he created a video that showed it. The humor and audacity of the video made people fall in love. Who doesn't wish they were the person who had thought to make a ridiculous "The Most Interesting Man in the World" video about themselves to demand a job? It got passed around, and shortly after the video was posted, Google contacted Matthew to set up an interview. So did several other major companies.[22]

The problem with embracing rejection is that it hurts. It feels like someone's saying you're not good enough, and you're going to be ready to react negatively. When someone says no, it feels like they're saying you're not good enough, and you're going to suspect that they're right.

Rejection isn't personal. It's not that you're not enough; it's just that you haven't refined your message enough to cleanly articulate who you are and what you have to offer. Matthew Epstein was exactly the same kid in his résumé and his video. He had the same skills, talents, and level of passion in both. He easily could have taken Google ignoring his résumé as a sign that he wasn't good enough to be on their team. He clearly didn't take the message that way. He fought. The minute you see that video, you can see the charm, creativity, and technical savvy it takes to succeed in tech marketing. He knew his product was solid; it just took some rejection for him to realize his marketing plan was entirely too conventional.

I like to think of rejection as the gamma rays in *The Incredible Hulk*. It's the stuff that gets shot at you to force you to mutate and grow and develop the powers you need to succeed. If you don't get a dose of it, you'll just keep going through life, doing stuff the boring, conventional way. You're never going to be impressive unless you need to be impressive, so why not put yourself in a situation where it's your only option?

Maybe what I'm saying is that life is like lifting weights. You need some resistance or you're never going to grow.

The people who have faced epic levels of rejection and persevered through them are the stuff of legend. Michael Jordan was cut from his high school basketball team. J. K. Rowling, Agatha Christie, and Margaret Mitchell all were told what terrible writers they were before they finally got the one acceptance that made them legends. *Anne Frank: The Diary of a Young Girl* got rejected fifteen times. *Anne Frank!* If Anne Frank's dad can live through the Holocaust, get fifteen letters of rejection, and still keep going, I think you can survive after a woman hangs up on you while you're telemarketing.

Another reason to embrace rejection is so you won't fear it. *MADtv* star Bobby Lee tells new stand-up comedians that "you aren't a comedian until you bomb one hundred times." He's not saying you have to have solid jokes or a great stage persona to be a success; he's saying you're never going to get solid jokes or a great stage persona until you know what bombing feels like so intimately that it doesn't scare you anymore.

About a year ago, Heather and I started looking for a house for ourselves. As well-known real estate agents, not just any house would do. It had to be a house for us, a place that could accommodate a growing family, and a representation of our style and taste as real estate agents. For a long time, looking for a place was in the backs of our minds. Then finally, the right place hit the market.

You cannot understand how perfect this place was. It was down in the flats, on the Beverly Hills–West Hollywood border—the kind of place where Heather and I could be close to all our listings and clients. We wouldn't be twenty minutes down a windy road in the Hollywood Hills; we would be in the thick of it. But the place was also secluded by a thick hedge, which would let us have a sense of peace and privacy. It was modern, sophisticated, and architectural. It was just a couple of blocks away from all the best shops on Robertson and from Petrossian, the caviar store that Heather can't get enough of. It was even two blocks away from the awesome Starbucks where

Matt and I had run into that NBA player (in chapter 4). It was our dream.

I made an offer on the place. I'm me, I knew what it was worth, so I made an offer just below that. The owners refused to even counteroffer. Suddenly, I was in that situation you never want to be in as a businessperson: I was trying to make a deal about something I was personally invested in. Heather was over the moon for this place. She wanted it really badly. But I also knew that if I paid too much for my own house, I'd always feel ashamed. This was also the opportunity for Heather and I to start a family and grow our lives together. I started negotiating against myself and made another offer for $50,000 more. The owners rejected it.

We were devastated. We weren't going to get our home. *Our* home. We'd been flatly, solidly refused and had to start looking again from square one. It was a pretty sharp rejection for a couple who was supposed to understand real estate pretty well and who was always telling our clients to not get emotionally attached.

Then, three months later, I saw a house on the MLS. Do you remember that house from chapter 9, the place just above Sunset that was desperately underpriced? I was able to walk into that place and close the deal because I could pay cash for it, because Heather and I still had the money that was supposed to go into buying our own home. We could have let rejection mess with our heads, spent too much money on our dream house, or gone running after a house that wasn't right for us just for the sake of having a house. Instead, we took the lump from the rejection and kept moving. That meant we had the money we needed to pull off a pretty spectacular deal, which made us a lot more money. So next time, when we're looking to buy a house for ourselves, we'll have a bit more of a budget to work with.

You can't let rejection scare you or confuse your goals. This is just like kicking the ball. If you knock on a door to cold-solicit a customer, you're going to be scared of what happens if they slam the door. Even when they don't slam the door, you'll be waiting for it. Once you've had a hundred doors slammed in your face, then you're free to just keep talking about whatever you're trying to sell. You know exactly how terrible that slamming door will feel, and you don't have anything worse than that to be scared of.

I'm not saying rejection is your friend. I'm saying it's your enemy, but you need to keep it close. You have to understand its secrets so you can outwit it. The more you understand rejection, the more you'll see the ways that you're actually asking for it. Embracing rejection is the first step in being assertive.

Once you've let a fair number of rejections blow through you—chilling you to your core, but not letting them dissuade you from your job—you might actually learn how to tell those who rejected you that they're wrong. I'm not talking about reactive, defensive insistence that you were right all along. I'm talking about being calm and confident enough to hear someone's rejection, notice a problem with its logic, and, without fear, try to clarify your message. Once you've absorbed so much rejection energy that it no longer scares you, people will be in awe.

Rejection is one of the harshest things we face in life. We all remember telling another kid in seventh grade we had a crush on them, then dealing with the self-loathing after they made it clear they didn't feel the same way. We're all trying to protect ourselves from being that kid again, so we create defense mechanisms. The thing is, you're not a kid anymore. You're a grown-ass adult who needs to start taking responsibility for your actions. You have to risk more than money in business; you have to risk your ego. If you want to be a big winner in life, you're going to have to put both of them on the table.

Rejection is fun for no one, but it shows you the way to keep going. It's a clear message about what you're doing wrong and it provides a few clues about what you can do to improve. Every time you get a rejection, aim to learn from it, to grow and be better. If you get to know rejection well enough, you might even be able to overcome it, because embracing rejection is the first step in screwing it.

17

Confront Your Weaknesses

We choose to go to the moon in this decade
and do the other things not because they
are easy, but because they are hard.

—John F. Kennedy

You're not going to be great at everything. We all like to imagine that person who has it all, for whom nothing is too difficult, and think how nice it'd be to be him. Like Ben Affleck. He seems like he has all the answers, right? Like maybe he's got the cheat codes to human existence, and he's using them to go through infinite lives, high-scoring every level. Or maybe that's just me.

The thing is, I'm not that guy. I dress nice, I make good money, and I have a smart, funny, beautiful fiancée, but I'm not someone for whom everything comes easily, and I've had to learn to confront my weaknesses head-on.

I've never been a particularly academic guy. I was always smart, and I always did solidly in school, but I just never loved learning stuff from books. I like learning from the real world—you know, where shit actually happens.

I realize now that I'm writing this *in* a book. Maybe I'm not that smart.

So throughout school I got decent grades, but by the time teachers started expecting me to write papers, I could no longer bullshit my way through classes. By college, I was on the football team, and thankfully I had a team of tutors ready to help me out. I used every single one available to get me through college.

You might be someone who thinks that pretending something doesn't exist makes it go away. If you want to learn from mistakes, you have to be honest about them.

The simple truth is that I managed pretty successfully to avoid academic work throughout school, and after I graduated, it didn't matter. It's not like I was gonna go get a Ph.D. All I needed to understand was houses, the people who wanted to buy them, and money. For my first four or five years of flipping houses, that was enough, but then I got that job selling mortgage refinances. To do it, I had to get my real estate license. To get my real estate license, I had to take a test.

It's like my life was one of those horror movies where I thought I'd totally killed the insane psycho—in this case, multiple choice tests. Then, just when I least expected it, I had to take one. I *had* to. There was no other option, other than quitting and going into another field.

I figured the test couldn't be that hard. I understood real estate pretty well. I'd bought several condos and houses, and navigated the system just fine. I couldn't really think of any practical part of the process I didn't understand, so I registered for the next exam. It was going to be a piece of cake.

When I got to the exam, the first thing I noticed was that we weren't in a classroom. It was a test; I'd figured we'd be in a class. That just made sense to me. Instead, we were in a big auditorium downtown. The place was packed with people, all looking very intense and focused. There was a lot of first-generation American work ethic in that room. I realized I might be out of my depth.

They dropped the test in front of me. Some of the questions made sense to me; some of them felt like Latin. Some of them *were* Latin. There's a lot of law in real estate, and I knew the practical applications, but I had never heard the technical terms. I sell houses in Beverly Hills. I don't need to know about riparian water rights, fees simple determinable, or escheatment, but that test sure seemed to think I did.

Here's the thing you need to understand about real estate law: it's *mostly* about *Downton Abbey* stuff. Seriously, there were questions about houses that can go only to male heirs. They asked about valuing the back forty of an agricultural field and measuring property "by leaps and bounds." Speaking a *Lord of the Rings* language would be more valuable to my business than this crap.

What I'm saying is that I failed.

This is the kind of stuff I had successfully avoided all my life. This is the kind of consequence I didn't want to have to face. When a person rejects my sales pitch, I can just go try to pitch another one. I couldn't charm a test. I couldn't make a test fall in love with exposed ceiling beams. In any other situation, I would have tried to wangle a way around the test, but this was the first time in my life I really felt like I'd found the thing I should be doing. As stupid as it sounds, houses are my passion, and if I had to figure out how to pass some test to be able to sell them, I guess I would have to buckle down and beat that test.

I heard about a crash course I could take in Marina del Rey where a guy would explain all the stuff on the test and coach me through passing. I signed up, paid the money, and showed up. It was a classroom. I had four years of great memories at Syracuse; none of them had involved a classroom. This place was not my element. I was sad that I was losing a whole weekend. I started to get mad at myself for not being better at tests and frustrated that I'd already sold lots of houses without knowing all this stuff. What I didn't think about was the test.

After completing the crash course, I took the test again. I had no more idea what was going on this time than I'd had the last time.

I wanted that real estate license, but getting it involved one of the things I'm worst at on this planet. There was no way to coast through, and I sure as hell wasn't going to try to cheat at this. The only option was to suck up and try. Try hard. At something I'm bad at. That's basically the least fun thing a person can do.

I went back to the crash course in Marina del Rey and this time I actually paid attention. It was hard for me, but I wanted this about as badly as I've ever wanted anything in my life. Turns out the intellectual guy running the class actually had some really great strategies for the test. He showed me trigger words to look for that would point me in the direction of the right answer. I busted my ass to learn everything I could in the class, then spent the next two weeks drilling myself to get the hang of it.

The third time was a charm. I passed.

We all have stuff we're bad at, and at some point in your career, you're going to have to deal with one of those weaknesses. Just like every couple of Superman movies, someone comes along with some Kryptonite, every couple of years your perfect job is going to make you do something you hate or are just terrible at.

One answer is delegation.

Like I've said before, I *hate* the busy work of real estate. I'm great at finding houses, showing houses, and closing deals, but everything in between those tends to bore me. At the beginning of my career, I got it all done, but the process always grated on me and stressed me out.

As soon as my business was big enough, I got myself a transaction coordinator. Her name is Amy, and she basically takes care of the parts of deals that annoy me. I *could* take care of this stuff. I have taken care of it in the past, but it takes more of my time and attention than it's worth. Some people thrive on attention to details like that. It's infinitely smarter for me to pay someone like Amy, who thrives on doing that kind of work, than to do it myself out of obligation.

As my business has gotten bigger, I've been able to bring on co-listing agents, people who complement my skill set and are experts in the business. That means people willing to be at the house for an inspection walk-through or spend the time inventorying furniture. These days, I have several co-listings in the San Fernando Valley. Driving from West Hollywood to the Valley is forty-five minutes on a good day. When traffic is bad, it can be terrible. I can't be spending that much time traveling for absolutely every incident in a sale. When I co-list, I can be there for the big stuff but be sure that someone responsible is there for the less important stuff. The more time they spend doing that, the more freedom I have to go do the parts of the job I'm good at. It's worth sharing the money.

If you really, really hate part of your job, the best answer may be to delegate that part to someone who will be able to do it better.

Sometimes it's just a question of temperament. I'm a people pleaser; I like being liked. My brother, Matt, has no such pretentions, so when we're negotiating, he plays bad cop while I play good cop. We're naturally suited to the roles, so we do a better job.

Delegation can't solve every situation, though. Sometimes you're going to have to do stuff that you're bad at.

Do it. Make it a priority. Care about it. Work on it. *Get better.*

Because you will. You can get better at anything if you try hard enough. If you've figured out a career you love, if you're putting yourself in situations to create opportunities, if you're working with people you like and respect and delegating most of the stuff you're bad at, your life is going to be pretty sweet. If you've got 2 percent of your job or 5 percent of your job that just sucks, that you're not naturally suited to doing, get over it and do it.

Organization can only take you so far. In any aspect of your life, at some point it will come down to tenacity. Can you keep fighting? Can you beat the odds, beat your opponents, and beat yourself? Can you win? Can you pass that real estate exam?

You can.

It won't be great. I didn't ace that test. I did what I needed to do, but I'm not a professional real estate exam taker. I'm a real estate agent. That's the part I excel at. That's where I'm amazing. The test was just an obstacle, and I overcame it.

Embracing your weaknesses isn't about saying you can change who you are. It's not like I passed that real estate exam and now I spend all my spare moments researching on the Internet and taking tests for fun. I'm just saying that in every aspect of your life you're going to be tempted to overemphasize obstacles. With any endeavor, it's easy to see the thing that is going to make it suck. Pretty soon, that's all you can think about and you're ready to give up.

So don't. Embrace your weaknesses. Just push through the pain, keep putting one foot in front of the other, and eventually, you'll get through it.

Nothing worth having is easy. I sincerely believe in making it as easy as possible. I live in LA, I have a pool, I wear custom suits. I'm no Midwestern farmer telling you that hard work with no reward is the only moral way of going through life. But running away from challenges isn't so noble either. Structure the best, most efficient life you can, and the stuff that's left, you'll just have to push your way through.

The reason you have to embrace your weaknesses is because the only other option is failure. If there's some task you're scared of, some obstacle that's intimidating you, you'll give up. If you're scared of failing, you're never actually going to succeed. The simple truth is, you probably won't fail. You'll probably just have to work a little too hard at something that's boring, annoying, or difficult. Get over yourself. Stop avoiding something that probably isn't that bad to begin with. Embrace your weaknesses.

18

Shift Happens

Progress is impossible without change,
and those who cannot change their
minds cannot change anything.

—**George Bernard Shaw**

Businesses change. You can build the best, most efficient business, but as time goes on, your industry is going to move and you're going to have to be ready to adapt your business to face the new challenges of the industry. Shift happens.

When George Eastman's company built the first consumer box camera in 1888, it captured a dominant position in the photographic industry. In 1975, when Eastman Kodak built the first digital camera, it had 90 percent of the U.S. camera market. The company was on top, and it was gently innovating to take advantage of new technology.

When's the last time you used a camera?

Since the 1990s, Kodak's business has seen a steady decline as photography in the United States moved from film to digital and from cameras to phones. In the late '90s, a share of Kodak stock cost around ninety bucks; now it's more like twenty. The market shifted dramatically, and Kodak didn't.

Fujifilm, in the exact same business, is doing fine.

Fujifilm started out in the same place. In the early 1980s, both firms saw that photography was going to be shifting to digital. Both also understood that the profits to be made from digital photography were way smaller. Kodak's whole business model was based on selling cheap cameras and charging people a huge markup on film. Digital cameras don't use film. Shit has changed. Fujifilm instead developed a strategy: make as much money as possible off the dying film industry, get ready for the advent of digital photography, and diversify its business.

Fujifilm figured out that a bunch of the chemicals it used for developing photographs were used to prevent oxidation, a thing that skin creams also need to do, so the company turned these chemical patents into a cosmetics line. It transitioned its film expertise into making optical display materials for LCD TVs. It produced digital cameras quickly and got them on the market.

Kodak was trying to do similar stuff, but its corporate culture was slow and clumsy. It never really figured out what to do with all its chemical patents, and it took forever trying to perfect its digital cameras. It tried to sell film cameras in emerging markets like China and didn't realize the booming middle classes in those markets would jump from no cameras directly to digital cameras. The company built an application to post and share pictures online, but in an old-school, Kodak way.

It was so trapped in its tradition and culture that it let little upstarts like Facebook and Instagram define the way everyone shares photos, because those companies understood social media. Kodak didn't. Its methods were old and unsophisticated, and it failed to understand that online media had a much smaller profit margin than the old film-reliant model. Kodak was very, very good at a business that didn't exist anymore.

Fujifilm, coming from a more competitive tradition, drastically reshaped itself, diversifying, cutting labor, and investing heavily in research. It wasn't a strategy that resulted in growth and dividends every quarter, but it's a strategy that kept the company alive and relevant.[23]

Markets change constantly. It's only the companies that have enough flexibility and energy to keep up with the markets that stay alive. It didn't matter how great of a buggy whip you built; once that first Model T rolled off the Ford assembly line, your business was destined for bankruptcy.

Just as conventional camera companies have been crushed by digital camera phones and social media, RIM, the company that makes BlackBerry devices, has found itself getting taken down by the very revolution it helped create. The company that held 54 percent of the North American market in 2009 now holds less than 3 percent.[24] There are lots of contributing factors—never coming up with an interface more sophisticated than a thumb-click wheel and keyboard wasn't exactly brilliant—but one reason that can't be ignored is social media.

Smartphones created the world of Twitter and Facebook. The opportunity to constantly be checking in with our friends changed how we thought and communicated, but RIM never contemplated that it should be managing its message in that world. Commentary about BlackBerry devices on Twitter and other social media were consistently mixed to bad, while the savvier teams at Android and iPhone created an online dialogue that encouraged and supported a positive image.

The lesson of BlackBerry is clear: if you're going to be shifting the market, you have to be aware of the changes you're making; otherwise, you might just step in a giant pile of shift.

My business is way smaller than something like Eastman Kodak or RIM, but I have to remain just as poised to correct the direction of the business when shift occurs in the market. Recently, the real estate market in Los Angeles has been blowing up. Demand for property is higher than it's been since I entered real estate, so the rules of the game have been slowly changing without anyone noticing.

A few weeks ago, I went for a listing meeting with an owner in Brentwood. He had a beautiful $10 million mansion. I was charming, I was engaging, I was everything you could want in a real estate agent, *and* I'm the guy on TV. I was pretty certain I'd landed the listing.

The guy called that night to tell me he'd given the listing to someone else. I could have just been pissed, assured him that he'd signed up for inferior service, and hung up, but that's not what aiming is about. It's about encountering your failures, looking at them, and learning from them. I asked him why he went with the other agent. He said that agent had offered to pay for staging.

See, this guy had a big, beautiful house, but it was empty. You don't want people to walk into a house that has nothing in it. Most people don't have the imagination to realize how great a place could be fully furnished. So owners usually pay for staging: renting furniture to make the place look like the opulent home it will one day be. Owners pay for staging, not real estate agents. Until now.

This isn't a term that the owner had brought up and I had refused. I am a guy who's willing to go in on a deal. This was just one of my competitors realizing how tight the market for listings is right now and being willing to do what it takes to get that listing. I have to respect that; more important, I have to *know* that. The market has changed, shift has happened, and I can no longer go into meetings with sellers without realizing something like who pays for staging is an up-for-grabs question.

Every new approach to real estate is a potential threat to my business, or a potential opportunity. Some new approaches may be irrelevant; some may be stupid. I'm not hiring sign twirlers or baking cookies to make the house smell nice, but I know that people do that. When I get outsmarted, outmaneuvered, or outstrategized, I have to learn how the agent who beat me did it so I can outfox them and everybody else next time. It's about aim.

A few years ago, there was this house up at the top of the hills on Curson Terrace. It was giant, had three buildings and a pool, and looked like a spaceship from the '60s. No one was going to want to move into that house, but buying it as a tear-down was a huge project. It was on the market for over four years starting at $6.2 million and didn't move at all. Then some guy I'd never heard of bought it for $4 million and resold it months later for $7 million with no remodel. I was *very* confused by what this guy had managed to pull off. Everyone on the street was talking about it. When he showed up at one of my open houses, I had to know what he'd done.

The guy, Nick, told me he'd spent the previous four months getting plans for a new house approved to replace the existing house. He didn't actually build the house, so he didn't have to front the money for the construction, but he did hand over an amazing vision to the buyers—everything they would need to be able to break ground immediately. That way the buyers had a new, modern design they could trick out with their own choice of fixtures and features, but a basic framework had already been approved by the planning board, which can be a long, tedious process, especially if you do not deal with the city on a regular basis.

It was a whole new approach to development. My industry had shifted, so I knew it was time to shift my ass and start playing this new game.

Over the past few years, Los Angeles real estate has been a constantly shifting game. New concepts like Nick's package deals are being innovated all the time. Another issue here is publicity. When a property goes on the market, it's very public, and all the information about a real estate sale has to be recorded with the county clerk, so it's all public record. For a gossip-hungry town full of home-owning celebrities, it's an easy source of stories. Some blogger posts some photos of a house, speculates that Dame Judi Dench is building a sex dungeon, and next thing you know, you've got a half-million hits.

Knowing these dangers exist in the market, agents have started privately listing houses off market. They're called pocket listings—those invite-only listings that many celebrity and wealthy individuals prefer due to privacy and exclusivity.

And in LA, once the famous people start doing something, then everybody rich or important wants to do the same, even if the tabloids aren't clamoring for information about them.

Recently, I was showing places to an A-plus-list celebrity couple who were looking for a new place. They only wanted to look at pocket listings, so I took them by a place in the hills that a friend was representing. It belonged to another A-lister, a young TV star. That's the thing about pocket listings: *everyone* involved is going to be somebody, hence all the secrecy. The couple passed on the place—it was too small—but I was interested. It was only a two-bedroom, but it was in a great location. I was in the middle of selling a place I owned, so I was considering buying this little two-bedroom for myself. I'd move in, renovate it, and flip it for a nice profit. Escrow on the other place I owned fell through, and I found myself in a situation where I just couldn't afford this little pocket listing and carry my mortgage on the other place. Shift happens. Things change and you have to be nimble. I strategized and sold it to Nick.

Nick bought the little two-bedroom place. He didn't move in. He cut down some trees (so you could see how good the view was), he put in a window (again, so you could see how good the view was), and he realized that the house was sitting on a full acre lot, so he had plans drawn up for a house that would fully actualize the potential of the space.

He's still getting plans approved, but once he's got all the architectural and legal stuff worked out, he's going to be able to sell that place for a couple million dollars in profit in way less time than it would have taken me to renovate it.

This time shift happened and I was the shift.

The world is constantly changing. That's what makes it fun. You can't just create one plan for attacking your goals and think that's the answer. You have to have a plan that can change and adapt as you learn from your mistakes but also as you learn how the environment is changing.

Whether it's business, sports, or relationships, anything you do exists in a dynamic environment with constant change. There are no rules, only guidelines that haven't changed yet. Always pay attention to the world around you, see what's changing, and when you get caught off guard, like I did with the agent willing to pay the cost of staging, *take note*. Try to figure out what that says about the alterations in your world, and look for other ways you might be ignoring the shift.

Because shift happens, and if you're not careful, the next shift could put you into the poor house.

19

Let Mistakes Open Your Eyes

There are no facts, only interpretations.

—**Friedrich Nietzsche**

I t's funny that human beings manage to get along with each other at all. There are over seven billion people on this planet, each with their own take on what's moral, what tastes good, and what temperature a room should be. Sometimes it feels like sharing a home with another person, even one as beautiful and supportive as Heather, is a full-time job.

The upside of so many different people having to share this planet is that we get the benefit of over seven billion people looking at the world in different ways. Everybody's got their take on what's going on. You can pay attention to other people's perspectives or you can ignore them; it's up to you. I think trying to see through someone else's eyes always makes me stronger. The more I see how any set of facts can be viewed in different ways, the more open and creative I end up being.

Mistakes are learning opportunities. They involve well-intentioned people not achieving the thing they tried to achieve. The more you understand what went wrong, the better you can be at deciding what the next step should be.

Every time you make a mistake, it's an opportunity to take a new look at stuff you thought you understood. Nobody goes into a situation thinking they're going to mess it up. You prepared wrong or you chose wrong or you thought you didn't need to work that hard to get ready for it. There's always something to learn about yourself and the world around you any time you mess something up.

All the people in America got to watch me make a pretty significant mistake in season five of *Million Dollar Listing*. I went to meet with a seller—a powerful Hollywood producer, Gary—who'd bought a place for $2 million, then spent ten years and a lot of money remodeling it. He'd had the place on the market for a year, but it hadn't moved, and he thought I could be the guy to change his luck. You know how I feel about luck.

Gary wanted to sell it for $4 million. He thought he deserved it for all the work and money he'd put into the place. It was a solid house: 7,000 square feet, five bedrooms, eight bathrooms, and a 27,000-square-foot lot, but it wasn't worth $4 million. You guys have heard me describe in this book a couple of places that just wouldn't move. Can you think about the common factor? Dark orange, Spanish-Mediterranean architecture. I have no idea why, but it was a huge trend ten years ago, and now no one wants those places, to the point of not even wanting to look past the design to see what could be done with the lot or house as a tear-down or renovation. I'd had my own Spanish castle that didn't move; I knew the dangers.

That house was telling its story in the worst possible way, so I told Gary that his best option was to drop the price by a million dollars.

Gary did not tell me to go screw myself, because he was on TV, but if you'd looked in his eyes while he was talking to me, you'd have seen that the message he was trying to communicate was "Go screw yourself."

I tried to make this guy understand. He was in a hard position. The house hadn't moved in a year. It didn't have qualities that I could get someone excited about it. But if we positioned the house the right way, we could get someone to take it off his hands. We could get someone to pay $3 million for that house. We could maybe even get three parties to come at us with offers, play them against one another, and get it up to $3.2. I told him this in the clearest possible terms, and he told me we probably shouldn't work together.

I went home, pissed at Gary for not understanding my point and pissed at myself for not understanding how to make my point. I sat down with Heather and we talked. I was looking for a little sympathy, but she didn't really see that as the moment to give it. She told me I was wrong.

Nobody loves houses more than I do, and I really try to understand their importance in a person's life. But I buy and sell houses every day. I have a clinical approach to the process. I talked to Heather about Gary and the house, and she convinced me that I'd gone into that meeting all wrong.

Gary had spent ten years of his life renovating that house. It had been a huge investment of money, time, and emotion. When I walked in there and told him it was worth a million dollars less than what he thought, I was beating down his dreams.

I had gone into that listing meeting, thinking of it as a time to articulate my strategy, to tell Gary what I was going to do to move that house. After talking to Heather, I started to look at listing meetings differently. Owning a home is an intense, emotional relationship. Most sellers, especially sellers living in their homes, aren't at a listing meeting to hear a crisply articulated strategy to move the house. They want to know that they can trust me. They're handing a huge investment over to someone they don't know. They need to see me as someone who will keep their needs in mind.

I shouldn't have walked in there and started by pushing him out of his comfort zone. I should have projected comfort, then talked him toward the hard realities of the market. I managed to salvage things with Gary, but that first meeting still got our relationship off on the wrong foot.

———————

A few weeks later, I ran into a similar problem with a client, John, who was selling a home in Manhattan Beach. This time he wasn't a guy who'd lived in the house for years. This was just a vacation place for a New Yorker. He had only owned it for two years and had probably only spent a few weeks in it, but my experience with Gary had made me gun-shy. I didn't want to overwhelm anyone at a listing meeting.

I went into the listing meeting with a different understanding, and a different goal. This time I was there to let him know I understood what he was trying to do and I could help him out. John had similarly unrealistic expectations about the value of his house. It was a gorgeous five-bedroom place just a block from the beach. It was full of brand-new custom fixtures and great design, but John wanted the place to be worth $4 million, and in that market, it just wasn't.

I didn't want to shock him, so I asked him to let me list it at $3.995 million, to get us away from the psychological shift that happens when you cross $4 million, and show it to some agents.

I knew what would happen, I knew how much the house was worth, but I couldn't be the person to tell John. I needed my colleagues to do it for me. I held an open house with piña coladas to set the mood and everything. I wanted to give this house the best chance to prove itself at just under $4 million. The agents came through and all told me what I knew: the price point was just too much in that market.

So I was able to go back to John and present him with the evidence. This whole process probably feels like a waste of time when I explain it this way, but Gary had shown me that it isn't. These guys aren't real estate agents. They don't know the market. They just know their own investment. I needed them to see the process so they could really understand the appropriate price points for their houses.

Every mistake is an opportunity to reevaluate the situation around you and try to see it in a new light. Aiming is about trying to not just solve your current problem but also see how that problem affects your worldview, and shifting it. You're not just aiming for one target; you're aiming to be better at hitting all the targets.

In this situation, the aim I took away was to remember that my perspective is limited and I need to look outside of it. It can be something as simple as remembering that the seller isn't a real estate agent, and I need to think about how he's looking at the sale. It can be as complex as the guy who saw people struggling to get plans approved for houses and started packaging lots with approved plans so construction could begin immediately. In each case it was simply about looking at facts that seemed like a failure and recombining them into a success.

When you mess up, your first inclination is going to be to *react*. You might assure yourself that there was no possible way you could have avoided the mistake. This move is to protect your ego. That's fine if you want to always be right, but I don't want to always be right. I want to win.

The only people who are always right are people who are comfortable lying to themselves. You can convince yourself that life is handing you outcomes that you can't control. I, however, clearly don't agree with this. I'm a guy who believes you make your own luck, so I also think it's your job to step back and examine situations that felt unlucky.

Another reaction is to get mad at yourself. That's just another way of avoiding an honest evaluation of the situation. It's creating stress where you don't need stress. The goal when you fail at something is to get past the emotion as quickly as possible so you can start looking at the situation as quickly as possible to try to find what you weren't seeing before.

It's not always going to be easy. Failure hurts. Growing hurts. It's like working out. Every morning when I get up and go into that gym, I know I'm going to come out a little sore and annoyed, but in the long run, it makes me strong. I can see the gym as a pain or I can see it as a tool to make me stronger and better able to face a difficult world. Aiming is making yourself stronger for all future challenges.

Aim to open your eyes. When you make a mistake, look at it from all angles. How did other people's perspectives affect the mistake? If you'd been more aware of how they were seeing things, could you have avoided that mistake? And try to see ways that this mistake is actually a success. Did you avoid getting involved in a deal that would have been more work and heartache than you could afford? Does this mistake set you up for another, better success?

If you're going to figure that out, you have to push aside your presumptions and see the facts in front of you with all the possibilities they may contain.

20

Not Every Failure Is a Mistake

Anyone who has never made a mistake
has never tried anything new.

—Albert Einstein

You're going to make mistakes. It happens. Your goal is to learn and grow based on what you learn from looking back and examining your mistakes. You're human; just make sure you're always getting better at it.

In the remaining chapters in this section, I'll focus on the importance of looking back on your failures and trying to figure out what went wrong so you can aim to avoid similar problems in the future. When you evaluate your failures, though, you won't always find a mistake. Sometimes you made the right, best choices, and things still didn't come together. If you're going to aim for improvement, you can't react to every failure with fear. You have to be smart. Aiming isn't about living in the shadow of your last failure; it's about being smart enough to know which failures you should be learning from and what you should be learning.

In 1999, a kid at Northeastern University in Boston built a program that made it really, really easy to share MP3 files between one personal computer and another. He built it all alone, creating a platform for music sharing no one had thought of before. His name was Shawn Fanning, and he named the service "Napster" after his gross hair that day.

Within days, hundreds of kids at school were sharing their music files. Within months, it had swept the nation, and by February of 2001, it had twenty-seven million users worldwide. One man at his computer changed how we get music. That's brilliant.

However, you'll note that I said he changed how we *get* music, not how we *buy* music. The people using Napster were, of course, sharing music without paying for it. The record companies and artists went crazy. This kid was costing them millions. He was *stealing* from them. Except that he wasn't. At that point, laws about ownership of music only dealt with things like the illegal reproduction of music. The laws had been written for a world of record albums, cassette tapes, and CDs, and no one knew if the laws about reproduction actually did apply to file sharing.

It was definitely illegal when people used Napster to download a copyrighted song and burned a CD of it, but Napster wasn't the one doing that, it was users, and Napster had no real way of knowing which songs were copyrighted, since users were doing all the uploading and naming the files whatever they wanted. It was the chaos of an approach to technology so new that there were no rules for it to break . . . until the lawsuits started.

In *A&M Records, Inc. v. Napster, Inc.*, all the big record labels got together and sued Napster, blaming the company for the copyright infringement it was helping at-home users commit. Napster pointed out that there were lots of very legal ways to use its service. The record labels didn't care, and they had the money for better lawyers. They got an injunction temporarily stopping Napster from doing business.

A group of eighteen intellectual property lawyers got together to file a friend-of-the-court brief when the injunction was appealed, pointing out, "The district court's ruling would ban a new technology in order to protect existing business models, and would invoke copyright to stifle innovation, not to promote it." Despite the consensus that federal copyright regulations didn't precisely criminalize Napster's activity, the courts shut the company down.

The real irony of the story was that Napster probably created more album sales than it squelched. While Madonna and Dr. Dre were complaining about their singles leaking early, Radiohead's album *Kid A* got leaked and downloaded a million times. Despite the fact that Radiohead had previously never had a top twenty hit in the United States, *Kid A* debuted at number one.

Napster failed. After the injunction left the service inactive for three months, the company tried to relaunch as a subscription service, but by that point dozens of copycat peer-to-peer file-sharing sites had popped up and the record companies were uncooperative about creating a music licensing agreement. By 2002, Napster was in Chapter 7 bankruptcy, and in 2008 what was left of the company was sold to Best Buy.

Napster failed, but can you really say it made a mistake? Shawn Fanning created a revolutionary technology in his ratty little college apartment. He launched it and it was an overnight success. He didn't do anything that was illegal or encourage clearly illegal activity. It was only after the company was a success that the feds decided it was illegal. Bigger, badder companies with deeper pockets and more connections were able to build businesses like iTunes, Pandora, and Rhapsody off the digital music revolution that Shawn had started, but can we reasonably expect that an eighteen-year-old kid should have been able to single-handedly recreate the music distribution industry from the ground up?

I'm sure Shawn has kicked himself a thousand times wondering how he could have done it differently. The answer, honestly, was that Napster was a failure, but it wasn't a mistake. I'm not saying there were no lessons to be learned. Napster, Inc., cofounder Sean Parker went on to help another college visionary, Mark Zuckerberg, turn Facebook into the most powerful social networking platform on the planet. You remember Sean Parker. He's the guy Justin Timberlake played in *The Social Network*. Not bad.

Napster wasn't the victim of failed vision; it was the victim of a world that wasn't remotely ready to understand a shift to digital music. It took the explosive boom of Napster's meteoric rise and fall to scare established players in the field into innovating.

You can't freak out because you fail. You have to try to be as objective as possible about ways you could have avoided that failure and ask yourself if those choices really would have been worth the costs.[25]

———

B ack in chapter 7 I talked about helping a billionaire toy manufacturer–turned–real estate developer who transformed a $9 million tear-down into a $17 million mansion but who then used a different real estate agent for the sale because he didn't like my persona on *Million Dollar Listing.* That was a really hard moment for me. It made me question my whole decision to do a TV show. It made me wonder if I've cheapened my professional reputation by being on a reality show. It made me rethink the whole process.

In 2010 I was just another real estate agent in LA. I sold nice houses in the $1 to $3 million range in good neighborhoods, but I wasn't the rock star I am today. I was doing everything I do now: networking, providing quality service, and making decisions with intelligence and confidence. I was succeeding, but on a smaller scale.

Then I got a call from an old friend who was a TV producer. He said that a company in the building he worked in did a reality show about real estate agents in LA, and they were looking to replace one of the agents on the show. He knew I was a real estate agent, because every human being who's ever been within fifteen feet of me knows I'm a real estate agent, and he had told them about me. They were interested.

I still remember the afternoon I drove over to meet with the producers. I was terrified. I was thinking about all the reasons they wouldn't be interested in working with me: I didn't have huge sales yet, I'd spent a fair amount of my adult life in other careers, and I'd made a big, significant mistake early on with that Spanish house in the hills. What if they asked me about that?

That's how losers think, so I stopped. I focused on what was right about me, about my work ethic, my intensity, and how damned good I look in a suit. I sat in my car in that parking lot and focused on being the Josh Altman I always want to be. This wasn't a time to be nice; this was a time to show them who I was.

I went in and told them I was a big deal. I was honest. Some people would call it arrogant, but I disagree. I was going into a show about salesmen and I was selling the best salesman I knew. I didn't give them the answers they wanted. I talked honestly from the heart about my philosophy of life and business. I walked out of there pretty certain I'd just come off like a pretty big asshole.

The next day they called. They wanted me to come back.

My parents were certain it was a terrible idea. My mom was so worried I would ruin my life by going on some show where I'd make out with a bachelorette I'd known for twenty minutes, have my balls blurred out in the shared bathroom, then get voted off by tribal council. She was thinking about the cheap, exploitative reality television that does exist, and I understand why she was worried. It's a mom's job to worry. It's my job to take risks, and I knew that *Million Dollar Listing* had a strong upside.

Million Dollar Listing is a great show, and I'd seen it give realtors a chance to show off their properties and skills to an audience of millions. I knew this was the boost my career needed to go to the next level. I listened to my parents, but I made my own choice. I decided *Million Dollar Listing* was worth it.

That toy maker made me doubt everything about going on the show. He caused me to worry that more clients would see the show and have similar negative reactions. I wondered if my mom was right and I would destroy my professional reputation by going on a network full of Real Housewives and celebrity chefs.

That was me reacting, not thinking. As soon as I got my emotions to settle down, I was able to look at the situation critically. I made the decision to go for it and chose from then on not to ever regret that decision because of what the show has done for me.

Million Dollar Listing has taken me to the next level. Through the higher profile work I've been able to do on that show, I've now sold a billion dollars' worth of real estate. The show gave me the chance to show the world the level of service and intensity I give to every deal, and people have been interested. It's brought me to the attention of dozens of great clients who like and respect my aggressive, disciplined approach to business. *Million Dollar Listing* changed my life.

So screw the toy guy. Yeah, he didn't like the way I did business on the show, but dozens more people with budgets just as big as his have been impressed by my work. If pursuing the toy guy's business would require me to give up being on the show, I would lose out on way more money.

And in the end, what he disliked was me. Reality show cast members can say all they like about editing making them look like creeps, but in my experience, what I do and who I am ends up on the show. I'm a tough-as-nails fighter for my clients. I may not be the nicest guy on the show, but I'm the one who's moving houses for the best prices.

While I'm thinking about it, I realize those Real Housewives have been pretty successful too, using their shows to launch businesses and acting careers. Those chefs have taken the exposure from *Top Chef* and turned their raw skills into successful, exciting restaurants that people are dying to go to because they already know and respect the chefs. In the same way that Shawn Fanning changed the way we get music, Bravo has changed the way we learn about fashion, food, and nightlife. It's changing the way we learn about real estate too, and I'm proud to be a part of it. Like I said before, when the market shifts, you have to shift with it.

So being on *Million Dollar Listing* may have cost me a client, but it's not a mistake, not by a long shot. I can look at that lost client and say, with confidence, he is just the cost of doing business in a new and constantly changing market.

When you look at a failed business venture, a fun party idea that didn't work, or just a networking attempt that didn't go as well as you'd hoped, look at what you did wrong, but also recognize that the problem might not have been you. Sometimes fate is stacked against you. Sometimes the opportunity isn't ripe enough. Sometimes you just catch someone in a bad mood. If you can't figure out a clear way you could have improved your chances, let go of it. Kicking yourself over failures isn't helpful. If you don't have a clear idea of how to aim, it doesn't help you at all to keep worrying about it.

Your goal is to find ways to use every failure to sharpen yourself into an even more capable decision maker. Your aim will help you calculate the best strategies to go into situations and act with confidence, but if a failure doesn't provide you with a clear aim, let it go. You're not living in the past; you're aiming for the future.

So keep going, keep trying, keep working. Don't let thinking about your failures get in the way of giving yourself more chances for success.

21

Success

A successful man is one who can
lay a firm foundation with the bricks
others have thrown at him.

—David Brinkley

This is a business book. I've got lots of stories in here about
people with innovative ideas who turned them into a lot
of money, and I've told you a lot of stories about myself that
centered on how much money I've made off selling houses. If
you want to make money, this book can help you, but what I've
really been trying to communicate in the book is a philosophy:
working hard at something you love will make you happy and
valuable to the people around you, and to yourself.

We want to feel good. It's the most basic, most fundamental
gut instinct. We seek the things that make us feel good: food,
alcohol, silk sheets, the sunshine on a beach in Mexico. We can

convince ourselves that more of these basic pleasures are what it takes to make us happy, that if we won the lottery tomorrow, we could get on a yacht, sail away with our new supermodel girlfriend or perfect boyfriend and a bunch of Dom Pérignon, and never be unhappy again.

But you kind of know that's not true. You also know you'd get bored or you'd get sunburned or you'd get in a fight with your new perfect boyfriend—Paul Rudd—and in some way your perfect life would turn into just life. A pretty *great* life, but one with ups and downs.

It comes back to what that guy Mihaly Csikszentmihalyi figured out in that study I talked about in chapter 3: people are most happy when they're engaged in an activity that taxes them, that a long-term process of engaging with and working on the skills you like to use is the thing that will make you feel most fulfilled. There will be problems, there indeed will be setbacks, and they'll hurt worse, maybe, than random yacht problems, because you truly love the thing you're doing. But those setbacks will make your eventual victories even sweeter.

I sell houses because I love to sell houses. They make money for me, and I hope to use the comfort and security that affords me to take care of Heather and my family as it grows. But the most important thing I'll give my children isn't a nice house or good schools; it's showing them what it's like to work hard at something you love and the rewards it can bring you.

My work ethic isn't a business strategy; it's a way of life. Every day I work hard and I get to see the real benefits I bring to people. I get to show people the houses they're going to build a life in. I get to find the right spaces for companies to grow. I have the responsibility to help ensure that dealing with the material ramifications of the loss of a family member is as stress-free as possible. Every time I get to do one of those things, whether it be one of the happy ones or the sad ones, I'm satisfied. On bad days, when a deal falls through or a client calls me up and yells at me for forty-five minutes, I'm satisfied, because I know my energy is going in the right direction and I'm capitalizing on my skills in a job that I love.

A couple of Sundays ago I got a call from a major movie star I have dealt with in the past. He said, "Hey, what's with this $55 million house I'm hearing about?" I told him how great it was, and I got a little excited, because he's one of the thousand or so people on the planet who could actually afford it. I got off the phone and told Heather that the client wanted to see the place. She said, "Oh yeah, of course he's looking for a new place. He got married."

That's what I get from doing my job right. His family is growing, and he's asking me to step in and help facilitate that process. He wants to go from his sleek, modern home to a compound where his family can enjoy some privacy. His life is evolving and he needs my help; that feels great. It doesn't matter that he is worth half a billion. (Okay, it matters a little.) What matters is that doing my job and doing it well enriches others' lives, and my own.

He's a major high-profile celebrity, so he didn't just want to see the place, he wanted to see it *now*. I had to call and get one of the biggest developers in LA to leave his tennis lesson so he could come and show us the place. It was a Sunday morning and I was feeling a little worse for the wear after a night out with Heather, but I had bigger things to worry about. I hopped into the shower, got into a suit, and headed up to the place. He didn't end up buying it, but I got to know that I'm a part of his life now, and as his life and family expands, I'll get to help find him the right place for that growth.

———

There was a time a few years ago, my mom called me up and told me she needed me to sell a house for free. I told her that I couldn't, that I was a businessman, my time was money, and I couldn't afford to waste time on this project. She said the four words I didn't want to hear.

"Josh, I'm your mother."

That's it. You can't ignore that. She's the one who gave birth to me, put Band-Aids on my boo-boos, and made me peanut butter sandwiches. I had to say yes.

My mom had friends in Boston whose grandmother was getting older and was ready to move into an assisted living facility. It was a stressful time for her; it was a stressful time for her family. They didn't need any more hassle; they just needed the house to move as quickly and efficiently as possible. My mom was trying to save her friends from some stress, and she knew her sons were perfectly suited to take care of it. I had to help out because it was the right thing to do, and because I owe my mom everything. Real estate isn't just about money; it's about lives.

———

It's also great to get to hand off to others some of what I've learned from ten years of experience and some really great mentors. Dodgers pitcher Brian Wilson seemed like just another celebrity client when I first worked with him, helping him find a lease. At that point, he was just about to win the World Series. He's a bearded, tatted up baseball player with a big personality and a bigger mouth. I found him a lease, closed the deal, and thought he was taken care of for a while, but Brian's career blew up and he was ready for something bigger. Five years later, he reached out to me to talk about real estate, because he wanted to potentially do some investing and developing himself.

I've been taking Brian around for a while now, showing him my process and introducing him to developers so he can learn about the business. He's thirty-two, and he understands that you can't pitch in the majors forever, so he's getting ready for the next chapter of his life. He doesn't want to just be one of Major League Baseball's best closers; he wants to be LA's best developer in the future. It's a beautiful thing: Brian's career grows, Los Angeles develops, and I get to help with the process and make some money off it. Not so bad. In fact, Brian recently closed on an incredible build opportunity in the Hollywood Hills that I sold him. Within the next two years, when completed, I'll be selling that same property for close to $20 million. Now that's a home run!

That's the other great aspect of real estate: helping a city to grow. Over the past ten years, I've been part of some major developments. Beautiful houses exist in the Hollywood Hills because I helped with the deals that made them possible. Recently, I got a call from Steve Levine, one of the major players in LA real estate. He told me that he'd been watching what I do, and he was impressed. He said he had an opportunity for me to work on a $100 million plot of undeveloped beach in Marina del Rey. Few things have ever left me as proud, awed, and excited as that moment. For all the good feeling that came from having my work recognized by someone as impressive as Steve, the thing I am most excited about is that land and what it could potentially become. It could be a five-star hotel, multimillion-dollar condos, or just one enormous mansion for Beyoncé, Jay-Z, and Blue Ivy. I don't know what it's going to be yet, but I'm so excited to find out. That's the kind of stuff that keeps life interesting.

Calculated confidence lets me make these big deals, but the real reward isn't the money; it's the sense of pride I have in knowing I'm good at something and that I'm getting better. Having something great is nice, yes, but being something great—that's the best.

Pride and confidence aren't about money; they are way more profound. One of my favorite business stories is about George Vlagos. When he was a kid in Chicago, his dad, John, a Greek immigrant, would make George come to his shoe repair shop and shine shoes. John had been trained as a cobbler back in Europe, but in the United States, a land of mass production and factories, his skills weren't that valuable. John made George come shine shoes so he would learn just how grueling a manual-labor job was and, hopefully, go to college to avoid having to do that kind of work professionally.

George went to college and became a teacher, just like his dad wanted, but he couldn't stop thinking about shoes. His dad had made such amazing shoes, and George had loved the process of making them. All the shoes George bought in stores were essentially disposable. They were intended to be worn for a few months, never quite fit right, and then be tossed aside for something else. So George did the thing his dad had never wanted him to do: he started making shoes.[26]

Oak Street Bootmakers' products aren't cheap, and they aren't mass-produced. George uses only meticulously sourced American products and American labor to make shoes the way his dad used to. Making high-quality, small-batch boots is never going to make George a billionaire, but it does make him happy. Every day he gets to do something he loves, he's good at, and that is hard. America isn't exactly full of new manufacturing businesses right now, but George is ignoring that trend and helping to remind us how great it can be to pay a little more for a high-quality American-made product. Oak Street Bootmakers will probably never be a huge financial success, but it is already a huge human success.

I want you to be a success too. Whatever you do, take it seriously, prepare yourself for it, train your instincts to understand it, trust yourself to make key decisions quickly, and when you make a mistake, figure out what the lesson of that mistake is, pick yourself up, and keep at it with newfound wisdom.

You have this in you. The world has probably taught you that you're not that special, that you're just another lady or dude working a job, raising a family, being pretty normal. You probably think of success as something reserved for the Zuckerbergs and Gateses of the world, but that's wrong. Average people do amazing things every day. In business, in technology, in everything, regular folks like you and me are inventing, innovating, and changing the way we live. Being smart helps, but relentless pursuit of a goal is the only way anything gets done. You can do it. You don't have to be brilliant, beautiful, or rich to be tenacious. You just have to start on a project and not let go of it until it's where you want it to be.

It's hard to believe in yourself. It's terrifying to try. We're all scared of what it will feel like if we try and fail, but when we do that, we're ignoring just how great it will be if we try and succeed. Not even succeed all the way, just advance, progress, and make our lives better than they were before. Little successes like that are what pride is built out of.

They're also what big successes are built out of. If you are relentless in your pursuit of your goals, your successes will add up. They'll outnumber your failures, and they'll start turning into something that looks like a big success. Human will is an awesome force: it's changed the course of rivers, ended empires, and sent human beings to the moon. If humans can collectively do such awesome things, just think about what you could do if you actually committed to trying instead of wasting your time doubting.

You've already taken a big first step: you finished this book. You believe in yourself enough to think you could use these tools to succeed, so do it. Consult your gut, figure out what you want, and write it down. Figure out what you can do to start moving toward that goal. Then every day always do something that will advance your cause. Fall in love with the steps it will take to advance your cause. It will take time, it will take work, it will produce heartache, but in the end, you'll keep moving in the right direction. Your confidence will grow, your ability to make smart, quick decisions will grow, and you'll feel good about yourself along the way.

I've gotten you ready. Now it's up to you to make your move.

Acknowledgments

First and foremost, I want to thank my incredible family who is always there for me and supports every decision I make. Without you I wouldn't be here. I always say the true key to success is surrounding yourself with the best. Well, you are the best.

To my brother Matt, you're the best brother anyone could ask for. The fact that I get to own a company and go to work every day with my best friend makes it the best job in the world. We've come a long way from that fraternity house we used to live in. We always knew we would make it in this town—we just didn't know exactly how. Thanks for paving the way in every aspect of life. I couldn't have achieved the success I have without you constantly pushing me along the way.

To Mom, you are the greatest mom in the world. Your loving support as the matriarch really keeps this family together and stronger than ever. It's nice to always know your mother's only a phone call away and happy to talk about anything, and I won't hold it against you that you told me not to do *Million Dollar Listing.*

To Dad, I guess you're not the only Altman in the family with a book now! And I didn't even have to be a Harvard professor. You're the smartest man I know, and what you have taught me about business, life, and public speaking has been invaluable.

233

To my fiancée, Heather Bilyeu, love you baby! Thanks for supporting me day in and out, and for putting up with me constantly on the move—whether it's filming, speaking tours, book writing, selling real estate, or any of the other crazy business. The support you give me allows me to accomplish everything in life I go after. Thanks for sitting with me for long hours pulling this information out of my brain even though I don't have the best memory.

To my grandparents Sidney, Sara, David, and Edith who all laid the foundation for the Altman family. I love you and miss you all.

To my dogs, Diego and Lucky, my other two roommates, you guys are the best dogs in the world for always giving me kisses when I come home after a long day and for putting a smile on my face.

Thank you to my wonderful agents Michael Broussard and Greg Ray, my manager Robert Thorne, and my writer Guy Brenan who helped me put the words on paper. Special thanks to HarperCollins who took a chance on me knowing it was going to be an uphill battle: Mark Tauber, Genoveva Llosa, Nancy Hancock, Hannah Rivera, Natalie Blachere, Suzanne Wickham, Kim Dayman, and the rest of the HarperOne team.

And to everyone at Bravo, including Jenn Levy, Shari Levine, Francis Berwick, Andy Cohen, and David O'Connell, who allowed me to be part of such an amazing network. And to all my friends at World of Wonder, the best production company to be part of, Randy Barbato, Fenton Bailey, Chris Skura, Todd Radnitz, Angela Molloy, Betsy Allman, Angela Berg, Shahram Qureshi, and Ray Giuliani.

Notes

1. Know Your Gut

1. Mark Prigg, "Trusting Your Instincts Really Does Work, Say Scientists. You'll Be Right 90% of the Time," *MailOnline,* November 12, 2012, http://www.dailymail.co.uk/sciencetech/article-2231874 /Trusting-instincts-really-does-work-say-scientists.html.

2. Know What You Want

2. Jari-Erik Nurmi, "Age Differences in Adult Life Goals, Concerns, and Their Temporal Extension: A Life Course Approach to Future-Oriented Motivation," *International Journal of Behavioral Development* 15, no. 4 (December 1992): 487–508, http://jbd.sagepub .com/content/15/4/487.abstract; and Katariina Salmela-Aro, Kaisa Aunola, and Jari-Erik Nurmi, "Personal Goals During Emerging Adulthood: A 10-Year Follow-Up," *Journal of Adolescent Research* 22, no. 6 (November 2007): 690–715, https://www.jyu.fi/ytk/laitokset /psykologia/henkilokunta/salmela_aro/jar303978.

3. Elizabeth H. Bishop, "Country House Revisited," (master's dissertation, University of Leicester, 2011), http://www.collectionstrust .org.uk/attachments/article/1249/country_house_revisited.pdf.

3. Fall in Love with What You Do

4. Ari Armstrong, "Mike Rowe's Excellent Career Advice," *Objective Standard,* May 5, 2014, https://www.theobjectivestandard .com/2014/05/mike-rowes-excellent-career-advice/; and Maia

McCann, "A Fan Asks Mike Rowe for Career Advice . . . He Didn't Expect This Response, but It's Brilliant," Distractify.com, April 29, 2014, http://news.distractify.com/people/mike-rowe-crushes-a-mans -hopes-for-finding-a-dream-job-and-i-agree-with-him-100/?v=1.

5. Mihaly Csikszentmihalyi, *Flow: The Psychology of Optimal Experience* (New York: Harper and Row, 1990).

4. Choose to Be Lucky

6. Richard Wiseman, "The Luck Factor," *Skeptical Inquirer,* The Committee for the Scientific Investigations of Claims of the Paranormal, May/June 2003, http://www.richardwiseman.com /resources/The_Luck_Factor.pdf; and Richard Wiseman, "Be Lucky: It's an Easy Skill to Learn," *Telegraph* online, January 9, 2003, http:// www.telegraph.co.uk/technology/3304496/Be-lucky-its-an-easy -skill-to-learn.html.

7. Michael J. Mauboussin, *The Success Equation: Untangling Skill and Luck in Business, Sports, and Investing* (Boston: Harvard Business Review Press, 2012).

5. Let Everybody Know What You Do

8. "Airbnb: How Does a Fast-Growing Site Expand Awareness of a New Product?" Twitter for Business, Success Stories, 2014, https:// biz.twitter.com/success-stories/airbnb.

9. Royal Young, "Kelly Oxford's Present Perfect," *Interview Magazine* online, 2013, http://www.interviewmagazine.com/culture /kelly-oxford-everything-is-perfect-when-youre-a-liar#_.

6. Wear the Right Uniform

10. J. V. Peluchette and K. Karl, "The Impact of Workplace Attire on Employee Self-Perceptions," *Human Resource Development Quarterly* 18, no. 3 (2007): 345–60.

11. Hajo Adam and Adam D. Galinsky, "Enclothed Cognition," *Journal of Experimental Social Psychology* 48, no. 4 (July 2012): 918–25, http://www.sciencedirect.com/science/article/pii /S0022103112000200.

12. Bettina Hannover and Ulrich Kühnen, " 'The Clothing Makes the Self' via Knowledge Activation," *Journal of Applied Social Psychology* 32, no. 12 (December 2002): 2513–25.

13. "Nancy Lublin," Wikipedia.org, last modified September 30, 2014, http://en.wikipedia.org/wiki/Nancy_Lublin.

14. Silvia Bellezza, Francesca Gino, and Anat Keinan, "The Red Sneakers Effect: Inferring Status and Competence from Signals of Nonconformity," *Journal of Consumer Research* 41, no.1 (June 2014): 35–54.

8. Get in the Game

15. J. Chambers and J. Luther, "Eric Edelson and Fireclay Tile: An Unusual Path to Entrepreneurship," Stanford Graduate School of Business, Case E490, December 18, 2013.

9. Screw It, You Got to See What Happens

16. Mary Riddel and Sonja Kolstoe, "Heterogeneity in Life-Duration Preferences: Are Risky Recreationists Really More Risk Loving?" *Journal of Risk and Uncertainty* 46, no. 2 (April 2013): 191–213, http:// link.springer.com/article/10.1007%2Fs11166-013-9161-0.

10. Always Have a House to Show

17. Daniel McGinn, "The Buzz Machine," Boston.com, August 7, 2011, http://www.boston.com/yourtown/needham/articles/2011/08/07 /the_inside_story_of_keurigs_rise_to_a_billion_dollar_coffee _empire/?page=3.

11. Your Gut Is the Godfather, Your Head Is the Consigliere

18. Leanne ten Brinke, Dayna Stimson, and Dana R. Carney, "Some Evidence for Unconscious Lie Detection," *Psychological Science* 25, no. 5 (May 2014): 1098–1105.

12. It's Not Finished Until It's Finished

19. "Extending the Product Life Cycle: A Kellogg's Case Study," Business Case Studies, 2013, http://businesscasestudies.co.uk /kelloggs/extending-the-product-life-cycle/introduction.html#axzz 3HCjYO7M7.

14. Remember the Big Picture

20. Andy Sternberg, "Audio Pioneer and Newsweek Owner Sidney Harman Dies at 92," LAist.com, April 13, 2011, http://laist .com/2011/04/13/sidney_harman_dies_at_92_arts_entre.php.

21. Ruud van den Bos, Marlies Harteveld, and Hein Stopp, "Stress and Decision-Making in Humans: Performance Is Related to Cortisol Reactivity, Albeit Differently in Men and Women," *Psychoneuroendocrinology* 34, no. 10 (November 2009): 1449–58, http://www.ncbi.nlm.nih.gov/pubmed/19497677.

16. Embrace Rejection

22. Robin Wauters, "Google Fails to Hire the 'GooglePleaseHire .Me' Guy," TechCrunch.com, September 7, 2011, http://techcrunch .com/2011/09/07/google-fails-to-hire-the-googlepleasehire-me-guy/.

23. "The Last Kodak Moment," *The Economist,* January 14, 2012, http://www.economist.com/node/21542796.

24. Michael Oleaga, "iOS vs. Android Market Share in North America: BlackBerry's Decline Gives Microsoft Windows Phone 3rd Place," *Latin Post,* May 16, 2014, http://www.latinpost.com /articles/12691/20140516/ios-vs-android-market-share-north-america -blackberrys-decline-gives.htm; and John Paczkowski, "Continental Shift: RIM Rapidly Losing Ground in North America," AllThingsD

.com, September 13, 2011, http://allthingsd.com/20110913
/continental-shift-rim-losing-ground-in-north-america/.

20. Not Every Failure Is a Mistake

25. Joseph Menn, *All the Rave: The Rise and Fall of Shawn
Fanning's Napster* (Joseph Menn, 2011), Kindle edition; and Richard
Nieva, "Ashes to Ashes, Peer to Peer: An Oral History of Napster,"
Fortune, September 5, 2013, http://fortune.com/2013/09/05
/ashes-to-ashes-peer-to-peer-an-oral-history-of-napster/.

21. Success

26. "Your Business," MSNBC, aired April 21, 2013, from
transcript posted on ark TV, http://livedash.ark.com/transcript
/your_business/5304/MSNBC/Sunday_April_21_2013/638302/;
"Natural Rough-Out Dainite Trench Boot," Oak Street Bootmakers
website, 2014, http://oakstreetbootmakers.com/footwear/natural
-rough-out-dainite-trench-boot; and "10 Inspiring Success Stories,"
Inc.com, last updated May 13, 2011, http://www.inc.com/ss
/10-inspiring-small-business-success-stories#2.

About the Author

Josh Altman is one of the most successful real estate agents in the United States, specializing in the luxury housing markets of Beverly Hills, Bel Air, and the Hollywood Hills. Josh's clientele consists primarily of A-list celebrities, professional athletes, business leaders, and high-net-worth individuals from around the globe. Josh has sold over $1.5 billion in real estate including the most expensive one-bedroom house in history, which sold for more than $20 million. At any given time he has over $350 million in listings.

Along with his older brother Matt, Josh created the Altman Brothers (www.thealtmanbrothers.com), a one-stop real estate firm that provides both buyers and sellers with their exclusive white-glove, VIP treatment. Josh is known for his ability to listen and understand his clients' needs, allowing him to continuously deliver above and beyond their goals and expectations. His personable and professional character allows Josh to build and maintain solid relationships, which explains why his business has grown mostly from referrals and repeat clients.

Since early in his career Josh has always been heavily involved in all aspects of real estate. While many know Josh as a high-profile real estate agent, few realize that he has found enormous success as a real estate investor. Josh has quietly built a fortune buying and selling real estate, with several of his best residential "flips" making him a profit of over $1,000,000 each. Josh now has a strong passion for teaching others how to achieve success in real estate (www.realestatesuccess.com) and believes that that anyone can follow in his footsteps to change their life and financial future through real estate, with or without a real estate license.

Due to Josh's impeccable track record of success, he was offered a starring role on Bravo TV's hit show *Million Dollar Listing*. His dynamic personality, humor, contagious energy, and love for the business have made him one of the most sought after speakers on the global circuit. His unique background allows him to connect with all ages, from lecturing at universities and college campuses around the country to the most demanding executive boardrooms. With over a decade of experience and huge personal success in the real estate business, Josh Altman has become a household name when it comes to the high-end real estate game. The breakout star of Bravo's *Million Dollar Listing* has brought excitement back into the real estate business.

Despite his busy schedule, Josh still finds time to give back to his community. He is very passionate about volunteering his time and money to support numerous charities and causes. Josh grew up in Newton, Massachusetts, and attended Syracuse University where he played kicker on the football team. While he was at Syracuse the team won the Big East Championship two years in a row playing in both the Orange Bowl and Fiesta Bowl. After college Josh did a short stint in New York City before moving out West to pursue his dream of real estate. Josh has lived in Los Angeles since 2003 and currently resides in the Hollywood Hills.